KANIKSU

STORIES OF THE NORTHWEST

KANIKSU

STORIES OF THE NORTHWEST

THOMAS F. LACY

Keokee Co.

PUBLISHING

SANDPOINT, IDAHO

Published by:
Keokee Co. Publishing
P.O. Box 722
Sandpoint, ID 83864
Phone: (208) 263-3573

Additional copies of this book may be ordered directly from the publisher for $11.95 plus $2 shipping, prepaid with your order. Credit card orders by phone or mail are also accepted.

ISBN 1-879628-06-6

Printed in the United States of America

For my sons
and grandsons

CONTENTS

ACKNOWLEDGEMENTS

KANIKSU IS A COLLECTION OF STORIES OF PEOPLE WHO LIVED IN the Kaniksu of northern Idaho and the Lolo of western Montana in the '20s and '30s; the homesteaders, the sourdoughs, the lumberjacks, the rogues, the rascals, the sweet people.

They are basically true stories. However, the memory does tend to enhance and rearrange events and times. But there was a Charlie Schwartz, a Dinty Murphy, a Jim Ward, an Old Man Williamson, an Elmer Henchel, a Ross Middlemist, a Dewey Duffel, and a Jim Low. Their lives were stories, and the stories should be told.

In the telling I have had the help and the support of my son Robert, who edited the first drafts and helped me to see and feel. Thomas Hunter, the artist, caught so well the feeling of the country in his illustrations. Frances Simmons encouraged me to publish the stories and found a publisher for me, Keokee Co. Publishing in Sandpoint, Idaho. I wish to especially thank Austin Raine, Daniel Simmons, Ross Middlemist and Thomas C. Lacy. And finally, I wish to express appreciation to Facts on File Publications, New York, N.Y., publishers of Carl Waldman's, "Encyclopedia of Native American Indian Tribes," 1988, for historic information.

Part One

STORIES
OF THE
KANIKSU

Chapter 1

THE KANIKSU

THE KANIKSU OF MY YOUTH WAS A LAND OF DEEP BEAUTY AND mystery. Time was before the white man came to change it that only the Kalispel Indians moved through the land with little trace of having passed. Their life had a correctness not often seen in the white world.

The Kalispel were a hunting and gathering people. Originally their homelands extended from northeast Washington across northern Idaho to western Montana. Their main villages were along the Pend Oreille River, but they came to the Kaniksu in the summer and fall for the great trout and whitefish spawning runs and the abundance of game and bountiful crops of berries. The Kalispel were a peaceful people, hospitable to all visitors to their lands.

The simplicity of their lives, though largely waning then in the '20s, left an aura on the land that filled me with a sense of peace and balance. I was witness to something great coming to an end, and I felt awe in their presence.

Some of my earliest memories are of the Kalispel in their wagons wending their way up the old West Branch Road to Priest Lake to fish for whitefish in the fall of the year. They sat erectly, proudly. The men wore soft, black domed felt hats, and the women wore shawls over their heads. Though they wore the clothing of the white man, their quiet dignity shone through.

On the flats to the south of what is now called the Dickensheet Road, lodgepole pine tepee poles stood in a small clearing in the forest near the old road. It was an overnight camping spot for the Kalispel on the long journey from their reservation near Usk, Wash., to the fishing grounds on Kalispel Creek where it emptied into Priest Lake.

At the north end of Luby Bay, there is a wide, white sandy beach beyond which a bushy point reaches out into Priest Lake. It is bordered by great, orange-barked ponderosa pines. In the early days, the forest was more open, and we often saw deer come down to the point to drink. We called this lovely piece of land "The Indian Camping Grounds," for there was evidence that they had camped and hunted there. We found flint arrowheads, thin flint awls for punching holes in leather, and flint scrapers for removing fat from hides. These artifacts had a profound effect on me. To this day I sometimes dream that I am walking the beach at Indian Camping Grounds and finding hoards of arrowheads. The number of arrowheads I found would indicate that this was an ideal hunting site; the deer standing in the water would have been vulnerable, easy targets.

As a boy when I would walk up the trail to The Indian Camping Grounds, I would think of the Indians and imagine I was walking on their trail. And probably I was. For though the Kalispel traveled largely by canoe — a canoe with sharply pointed bow and stern that sloped down to the water — they surely left trails around Priest Lake. They must have traveled widely throughout the region, for I have found arrowheads as far north as the upper lake.

There is a rocky headland at the northern extremity of Kalispel Bay across from Kalispel Island. It is called Indian Picture Rocks, for on it are petroglyphs of animals and humans left by the ancient ones over 10,000 years ago. The Kalispel called the ancient ones the NoQuosh'Kol. I am drawn to these paintings at least once each summer and always view them with wonderment and awe that any work of man can so long endure.

Though the Kalispel have long been gone from the Kaniksu, I am often reminded of them. Their mark still remains on the land. There is Kalispel Bay, Kalispel Island and Kalispel Creek. And there is Papoose Island and Indian Creek. The vast forests that stretch across the Idaho Panhandle bear the name they gave it, Kaniksu.

Sometimes when I drive up the new highway to Priest Lake, over the High Bridge and onto the flats, I think of the tepee poles. I think some day I must stop, walk up the old West Branch Road, and see if the poles still stand. I think, if they have fallen and only a few decayed pieces remain, that they should be replaced, and the blackened fire stones that once rested in front of the poles should be found and replaced in a circle. And a marker placed with the words inscribed on it ... "The Kalispel, a peaceable people, once camped here."

Chapter 2

OLD MAN WILLIAMSON

OLD MAN WILLIAMSON WAS THE FOREST GUARD AT LUBY BAY IN the early '20s, a white-haired, crusty old bastard. He was the kind of man who owned an Airedale — a bear-hunting, fighting bully.

Every morning about 9 o'clock Old Man Williamson and Scar would walk past our cabin on fire patrol. Scar pranced ahead like a prize fighter doing his roadwork, challenging any and all dogs to go a few rounds with him.

On Tuesdays Old Man Williamson made a twenty-mile fire patrol through the southern part of his district, and on Thursdays he made a twenty-mile fire patrol through the northern part. On the other days of the week, he would walk up Lookout Trail each morning to two rocky promontories on a ridge at the south end of the bay and, if it were hot and dry, again in the afternoon.

The two promontories were called Lookout One and Lookout Two. It was a two-mile round trip, not too difficult for children.

Occasionally he would allow sister Jeanette and me and the Robinson and McWilliams children to tag along. He would admonish sternly, "No running nor horseplay on the trail. Walk quietly and slowly, and perhaps we'll see a fool hen or a deer." He was a man who inspired respect, and we'd be quiet in hopes of seeing wild animals.

From the lookouts, we looked down on people walking and swimming and the boats drawn up on the beach. We'd marvel that they looked so small from that height. We could look into Kalispel Bay to the north of Luby Bay and down on Kalispel Island and little Papoose Island and Baritoe Island. It was a whole new perspective and feeling for us, like the first time we skipped or jumped or turned a somersault.

But these were the few times that the sunshine of his soul shone through the dark clouds he wore. I do not recall him smiling or joking or stopping to chat with my parents nor waving as he walked past each morning. He was a loner and satisfied to live within himself.

His job was finding forest fires. If they were small he put them out himself. If they were large, he reported them to the ranger district headquarters in Coolin on his crank telephone. Jim Ward, the district ranger, would then send fire fighters to put the fire out. If the fires were in the backcountry, they could become quite large before the fire fighters could get to them. Occasionally a fire would burn out of control until the fall rains put it out.

The guard station where Old Man Williamson lived was once a houseboat, now drawn up on dry land. It rested on large logs. There was a tiny porch at the front. Off the porch was a pole from which the American flag flew. The building was painted dark brown with white trim and looked official.

When Old Man Williamson and Scar were off on patrol, we

could peek inside but never had the courage to go in. It was dark and forbidding like the man himself. There was a large, cast-iron cook stove along one wall with bake oven and warming oven above in the single room. A sourdough can rested on the back of the stove. Beside the stove was a bucket of water with a long-handled dipper sticking out. Often he could be seen to walk out on his dock, dip a bucket of water and return to his house. The water in Priest Lake was so pure and clear, you could drink it.

There was a small dining room table and two chairs, rough-hewn benches and stools in the room. In one corner was an iron cot and in another corner was a rough-cut desk where I imagine he made out and kept his reports. There were a few kerosene lamps with glass oil bowls and glass chimneys. The floor was worn but scrubbed clean. The whole was neat — neat as the man was about himself.

At the time, I had a Boston bulldog, a little mind-your-own-business kind of dog. Buddy was a warm, friendly little fellow and my best friend and constant companion. Every time he and Scar would meet on the trail that ran along the lakeshore, Scar would growl and challenge Buddy to a fight. But gentleman that he was, Buddy would ignore the bully's cheap shots.

One day Scar, after sniffing Buddy fore and aft, jumped him and forced Buddy to the ground. Buddy sank his teeth in Scar's throat, but Scar being larger and stronger shook him off, and they tumbled end over end to the water's edge.

Father, hearing the fighting, rushed out of our cabin and shouted, "Damn it, Williamson, call off your dog. Buddy's no fighting dog."

But Williamson shot back, "Let 'em fight it out. It's been a long time coming."

Father picked up a piece of driftwood and tried to force the two dogs apart. But he couldn't separate them, and he couldn't pull the two dogs apart without getting bitten. Scar forced the fight into the water and held Buddy under water until he went limp. Father waded in and pulled Buddy out, carried him in his arms up to the cabin and wrapped him in a blanket. Buddy was still breathing, but he couldn't eat when Mother offered him some warm milk with toast in it.

The next morning when I called for Buddy, Father took me out to a small copse of trees behind the cabin and showed me Buddy's grave. "Tommy," he said, "Buddy died during the night."

"Why did he have to die?" I sobbed.

"He fought bravely, but his heart must have given out, Tommy."

He didn't mention that it had all been senseless and cruel and Scar was a vicious brute and Williamson not much better, for I was too young to understand.

That Buddy was brave, I could understand. I never wanted to forget him, so we built a cross from two boards and carved his initials on it and pushed it into the soft earth. We picked some Indian paintbrush flowers, blue lupine and white daisies, put them in a can filled with water from our old, red hand pump and placed it on his grave.

Old Man Williamson continued to walk past our cabin every morning on patrol. He did not apologize nor say he was sorry for Buddy's death. He held the fire guard job for a few more years and then retired to his homestead at the outlet of the Priest River to the west of Coolin. He built a few cabins and lived comfortably on the rental income and the produce from a small garden and orchard.

We heard little of him until the summer of 1926. That was a dry year in the Kaniksu, and lightning from an August storm that moved in from the west started several fires. One fire north of Priest River took out a lookout tower and threatened the town itself.

Another fire that had started in the mountains to the west of us was threatening Kalispel Bay. Smoke from the fire was so thick we couldn't see across Priest Lake. Papoose and the other islands were blotted from view. The smell of smoke was heavy in the air.

A strong wind came up and the fire burned out of control. In the evening, Jim Ward came down the bay and warned all of the summer people that the Kalispel Bay fire would take that bay out and was headed for Luby Bay.

"We've built a trench from the lake north of you over the hills to the West Branch Road and have started a backfire. We hope it will burn everything between the trench and the main fire and pinch it off.

"But there is no certainty we can stop it. So take what you can in your boats and bury the rest in the sand. Then go down to Fred Williamson's. You'll be safe there."

Williamson. I still hated the man for what he had done. I could still hear him say, "Let 'em fight it out." And I could still see Scar holding Buddy under the water. I detested the thought of staying with the man. I looked to Mother for some answer, but she was already taking precious personal items out of bureau drawers, and seeing me standing there said impatiently, "Get busy. Bring boxes and the suitcases out of the shed to put things in. Pick out things you want to keep."

"You've forgotten Buddy," I cried, tears welling up.

And then she came and put her arm around me and said, "No, Tommy, I haven't forgotten."

"I hate the man," I said. "I don't want to stay with him!"

"Tommy, we mustn't carry hate in our hearts or we become like Mr. Williamson," she said softly. "We must try to understand. Perhaps there was a great sadness or hurt in his life that causes the anger he carries. We all loved Buddy. But we cannot let our love for

Buddy and his death become a cancer in our souls that spreads."

Then she brushed the hair back on my forehead and the tears away that had gathered on my cheeks, kissed me and said, "We must try to understand the Williamson's and forgive and forget. And now we must get back to packing. It will soon be dark."

We put our most prized possessions in the Mary, named after Mother. Mattresses, cooking utensils, canned food, furniture we placed in several piles on the beach, laid blankets over them and covered the piles with sand.

The sun was setting as we cranked up the Elto outboard motor on the Mary and headed out into the bay. We turned for one last look at our beloved cabin, and there standing among the mounds were Mike Luby and Charlie Robinson, two other cabin owners, their heads bowed, their hats held over their hearts. It had the appearance of a graveyard.

When we drew even with the point at the Woodrat Mine, we could see into Kalispel Bay. It was all ablaze, fire boiling up and black smoke reaching into the sky. The fire had reached a height of land above the beaches, and as we watched, marched down the slope to the cabins along the shore. The heat was so great that cabins exploded into flames, and for a few brief moments the windows stood out black and then the cabins disappeared.

The fire had crowned and was moving at high speed among the tree tops. The only things that could stop it were the waters of Priest Lake and Jim Ward's backfire.

We sat watching, mesmerized by the fire's awesome power — the towering swirling flames, the shower of orange sparks that reached far out into the bay, the reflections of the fire on the waters surrounding us. A flotilla of boats had gathered, refugees from both Kalispel and Luby Bay, watching the fire.

Then Mother said, "We must leave before it becomes too dark

to get through the shoals in front of Mr. Williamson's." The water there was not over two feet deep and mined with large boulders that could tear the bottom out of a boat. As we approached the shallows, Mother cut the speed of the motor to where we were scarcely moving and said, "Tommy, your eyes are sharp. Crawl up on the prow and guide me through the boulders." I felt so proud of the trust placed in me that I temporarily forgot about Old Man Williamson.

In the gathering darkness, the boulders were vague dark shapes against the lighter sandy bottom of the lake, and here and there larger boulders broke the surface. I would shout "left" and point to a submerged boulder or "hard right." The Mary was heavily loaded, rode low and sluggish in the water. Once we bounced broadside off a rock, but her sides were strong, built of narrow strips of inch-thick cedar and no damage was done.

As we drew near the outlet, the water deepened and we could feel a current building up as the water rushed to leave the lake and enter the riverbed. There was a rapids but a short distance down-river. To the left was Old Man Williamson's dock. The trick was to cut across the current and at the same time avoid being sucked into the rapids below. Mother gunned the motor, made a sharp left across the current and swooped into a landing alongside the dock.

We had been so engrossed that we hadn't noticed Old Man Williamson standing on the dock watching us. He tied the Mary up and then said, "Well done, Mrs. Lacy. Welcome to Pawnee Ranch."

There was a touch of warmth in his voice, and he even smiled, something we had never seen before. Mother smiled up at him and said, "Well, thank you Mr. Williamson. Did Jim Ward reach you?"

"Yes, he said you were coming. The cabins are taken, but I can put you up in my ranch house. There is a bedroom for you ladies, and I can put a cot in the living room for Tommy."

I didn't like him calling me Tommy, nor implying that we were old friends. I didn't like staying in his house, but Mother said, "That is very kind of you. Thank you."

He reached down, helped Grandma then Mother then Jeanette onto the dock. I jumped out before he could help me. His house was set back from the beach on a bench that had a long view up the lake past Baritoe and Four Mile Islands all the way to Lookout Mountain. There was an open porch across the front and immediately within a large room that combined a living area in the foreground with open kitchen and dining to the rear. The ceiling was low, and I remember the room being warm and comfortable. There was a fireplace and on the walls deer racks and grouse fans. Before the fireplace was a large black bear rug and some of the furniture was upholstered with cowhide from which the hair had not been removed. The cowhides were tan and white, and black and white. There were even white curtains at the windows.

Beyond was an open hall with bedrooms on either side. One of these he showed to Mother, and I heard her exclaim, "White sheets and such quaint down comforters. You didn't make these yourself, did you?"

"No, they were handed down."

He told us to make ourselves comfortable, and he would remove the things from our boat and put them in our room. After he left, Grandma said, "He is so different. Kindly. I felt he was pleased to see us and have us here."

"Yes, I noticed it too. He's a different man than he was two years ago. Whatever it was, I'm happy it's over for him," Mother said.

After retrieving our things, he set up an army cot for me near the fireplace. "Where you'll be warm, Tommy," he said.

I hadn't seen Scar and I asked, "Where is your dog, Mr. Williamson?"

And he replied, "He was killed by a grizzly we ran down. About a year ago it's been now. Buried him out back under an apple tree he liked to lay under when it got hot in the summer. I marked the spot with a cross."

"I marked Buddy's grave with a cross, too," I said. "We put flowers on his grave."

"I'm sorry about that, Tommy. I saw your cross back there, but I could never bring myself to say anything. I don't know why ... I don't know why." And then he turned and slowly walked down the hall.

The next morning I awakened to the smell of bacon frying. Mother, Grandma and Jeanette were seated at a long, picnic-type table, pancakes stacked before them topped with a fried egg and garnished with thick slices of ranch bacon. I hopped out of bed and over to the big wood-burning cast-iron stove where Mr. Williamson was frying sourdough pancakes on a large, black cast-iron griddle. There was a chill in the mountain air, and I reached out to the fire to warm myself. I watched him grease the griddle with a piece of bacon rind and pour dippers full of milky white sourdough onto it that puffed up to plate size pancakes. He handed me a stack with the bacon and egg and said, "See if you can wrap yourself around these, Tommy."

At the table was a bowl of raspberries from his garden for me and a blue enameled metal pitcher of thick cream to pour on them. "We have reached your father, and he is driving out from Spokane later today to pick us up," Mother announced when I sat down. "We'll be going back with him for a few days until the forest fires are under control. We still do not know whether the fire reached Luby Bay or not, but Mr. Williamson thinks Jim Ward will stop it."

"Do you really think he can stop it?" I asked him.

He came over and put his hand on my shoulder and said, "If Jim Ward can't stop it, no one in this whole world can stop it. He's the best. I'd put money on it he'll tame that fire."

"Thank you, Mr. Williamson," I said, near tears from loving Priest Lake and the cabin so.

Later that afternoon we heard Father's horn across the river from us. Mr. Williamson went over in one of his boats and brought him back. Father told of having encountered another fire a few miles out of Priest River. The fire had reached the road and smoke hung in the air, and from time to time he saw orange red spots of fire just off the road. Finally he was held back by fire fighters who said there were still sparks coming down on the road ahead.

A Forest Service truck came at last down-road from the burned-over area. By that time there were cars backed up far behind Father — other anxious husbands. The driver of the truck said they had the fire under control, and he would lead them to safety beyond the burn.

Father moved us to Spokane. Jim Ward stopped the inferno with his backfire and saved Luby Bay. We returned to find Kalispel Bay devastated. The first day back we took a boat ride over to view the damage. Black snags stood straight and tall out of the black-ened earth. In the great waste, a few pockets of green, fire-resistant cedar survived where it was damp. The shiny tracks of the Dalkena Logging Company's narrow-gauge logging railroad snaked starkly up the valley of Kalispel Creek. Along the bay a few fire-whitened stone fireplaces and twisted metal beds and cast-iron stoves was all that remained where once cabins stood. When we turned our Elto Motor off, a quiet lay on the land. There were no signs of life, not even a bird.

We stopped at the Outlet over the years, when we were out for a ride in the Mary, to see Mr. Williamson. He always offered us oatmeal cookies from a crockery cookie jar and chilled milk from a milk bottle he kept in a spring-fed, wooden trough at the back porch. In the early days, the Indians had called him Chief Pawnee White Eagle because of his snow white hair. He liked to have the children call him Pawnee Fred.

Chapter 3

THE GENTLEMAN

ON THE OPEN FLAT EAST OF NEWPORT THE ROAD TO PRIEST RIVER
lay straight and dusty, the deep dust on its sunbaked surface billowing and trailing far behind as our car sped over it.

The day was a typical late September day. It was warm. The sun
burned down through a blue, cloudless sky. Our Elgin touring car
was open to catch the breezes. Father and I were in the front seat.
In the back seat were Mother, my sister Jeanette and our beloved
Aunt Grace, Mother's sister.

Father, his foot pressing the gas pedal to the floor, coaxed the
last bit of speed from the car's engine. His mind was set on gaining
a few minutes to add to the few precious hours he'd have at our
cabin at Priest Lake. We were on our fall pilgrimage to the lake,
and our stay would be brief. We had left Spokane at noon this particular Saturday and would have to return late Sunday.

Father sat stiffly in full suit and tie. He was conservative, correct. He always wore a gray or navy suit and tie, even in the evenings at home. He was a dedicated family man. He was concerned with my learning the things he considered important for success in life. "Success" was one of his favorite words, as was the word "power." The power of words, the power of observation, the power of concentration, all were synonymous with success.

He often would say, "Let's take a walk," or, if we were at the lake, "Let's chop a little kindling," or "Let's go row the boat." And then he'd talk about the latest books: Hubbard's "A Message to Garcia," Vash Young's "A Fortune to Share," Mary Andrew's "Abe Lincoln." I called these talks the "chopping block lecture series," "the walk lecture series" or "the rowboat lecture series."

Normal in most ways, he did have one obsession — speed. He was obsessed that no car should ever pass him. He would use every trick in a race car driver's book to prevent this from happening; the weave, the swerve, the squeeze, intimidating the opponent, forcing him to pull over for his final burst of speed and swoosh by.

Mother and Aunt Grace were either utterly without fear or were inured to his way of driving, for they were chattering away in the back seat, stopping only now and then to catch their breath. From time to time their voices would trail off to a whisper, annoying Father, and he would grumble, "Who are you Cherry Sisters talking about now?" Who the Cherry Sisters were, was all part of the mystery of grown-up talk and of insufficient interest to invite inquiry from a boy of eight. I suspect, however, that the Cherry Sisters were actresses, and like the sweet little old ladies in Arsenic and Old Lace, carried secrets.

And yet, Mother and Aunt Grace were two of the dearest ladies who ever lived. Aunt Grace was our favorite aunt. Not because she made the largest chocolates — candy bar size — at Christmas, but because she made each of us feel special to her. She was the liberal one in the family, introducing sister Jeanette and me and cousin Chandler and Margie to the delights of bubbly apple cider that had frozen and "worked" on her overflowing back porch. Being a maiden lady she was the one designated to care for our grandmother.

And then there was Mother. She was a home-making, loving lady in an apron always ready with mercurochrome for skinned legs and hugs and kisses for hurt feelings accumulated on the neighborhood playing fields. She stood up to the police, backing them down when they had the temerity to suggest that Jeanette and I had been involved in the near burning down of old man Isaac's barn or climbing on freshly laid brick walls while exploring the new houses going up in the neighborhood. All the time we were hiding under our beds as we had been told to do. She read to us from the Bible each evening as we huddled around the dining room register, warming up prior to plunging into bed on the frigid back porch. Grandpa Chandler died of consumption, and we were compelled to brave sub-zero temperatures with bed warmers on that torturous back porch as prescribed by the medical giants of the day.

Sister Jeanette, though six years older than I, always allowed me to tag along with her gang. She charmed me into thinking I was the bravest, toughest kid in the neighborhood and granted me the honor of being first in everything. First to jump off the apex of the garage in a parachute we made from a bedsheet and receive a badly sprained ankle. First to storm the enemy parapets in the "Great Mud War" and get a load of mud in the face from the giant sling shots mounted on the other side of Tekoa Street. First to step up to the plate and get a feel for the new pitcher and promptly get bean-balled. It was a great surprise to me in later life when she became so active in the Presbyterian Church.

It was Jeanette who first saw the black dot far down the highway that soon took on the shape of an open touring car with top down. As we drew closer to the car we could see that the hood was up and two men were peering into the engine. Father, I'm sure, was sorely tempted to go on — lose not a moment — but the rule of the road at that time was to stop for anyone with car trouble.

He slowed and pulled to a stop behind their car. One of the men wore a chauffeur's uniform. But from the bulk of him, the puffiness around the eyes and ears, the ham hands, he seemed to be more than just a chauffeur.

The other man wore navy serge trousers, a crisp white shirt and black tie. I remember him as being tall, blond and good looking. He walked over to our car and introduced himself. Close up, we could see that the shirt was french cuffed with diamond cuff links — a man out of place in this wild country.

He smiled warmly and said, "I'm James Tracy. Surely appreciate your stopping. Have had nothing but trouble with this Maxwell."

"I'm Bert Lacy. Anything we can do for you?" Father asked. "Get help, drive you back to Newport?"

"No, no," he replied. "I've already sent word to my garage. If you are going as far as Priest River, though, I'd appreciate a ride. I'm in a bit of a hurry to get there."

"Of course, glad to oblige," Father replied.

"First, let me get my suit coat and have a word with my chauffeur. Only take a minute."

Father told me to get in back, and I squeezed my skinny frame between Mother and Aunt Grace. "My what a gentleman! Handsome, too, don't you think, Grace?"

"Mmmmmmm ... yes," she said demurely. "Tracy ... Tracy ... you don't suppose he could be related to our minister do you?"

"Yes, he does have that same nice, polite manner doesn't he," Mother replied.

Tracy and his chauffeur seemed to be arguing over something, but whatever it was they soon came to some agreement. Tracy lifted his coat off the back seat, slipped it on and returned to our car.

We had gone but a short way when a car with several men in it pulled abreast of us. As usual, Father floored the gas pedal, determined not to "eat their dust" as he liked to say.

The other driver was just as determined to let us eat his dust, and off we raced down the highway.

"Give her the gun," Tracy cried. And in rising enthusiasm, warming to the race, "Run him into the ground."

We raced neck and neck, both drivers leaning tensely forward, striving for some small advantage. Father tried the weave and swerve. Jeanette screamed. I shouted, "Don't let him pass us." Mother cried, "Bert! For heaven's sake slow down."

But he hung on grimly, edging ahead slightly. And then the road took a sharp left. Both drivers hit the brakes to prevent floating off into the open prairie. Dust boiled over us as we sliced around the curve. Being on the inside, the other driver had the advantage. He recovered faster and moved half a length ahead, and the race was over. The dust was so thick it completely shut off Father's vision, and he had to stop or run off the road.

Tracy, apparently sharing with Father the humiliation and pain of defeat, offered consolation, "We'd have had them but for the curve. We were ahead going in."

Mother whispered to Aunt Grace, "We're lucky to be alive."

Ignoring the Cherry Sister's whisperings, Father said to his new found partner, "We just ran out of road. I had him cold."

The road left the open prairie and entered the forested hills that lay along the south bank of the Pend Oreille River. Pine and cedar and hemlock crowded close upon its shoulders cutting off the sunlight.

There were deep ravines, the road winding with frequent hairpin curves. It was cool, quiet and foreboding. At the Washington-Idaho border, the car that passed us was blocking the road. Standing beside the car were three big, grim-faced men. Two were armed with sawed-off shotguns. It looked like a holdup.

There was no alternative but to stop. They'd laid a neat trap; the road was too narrow to squeeze around the blockade, too late to turn back.

We waited, tensed, as the largest of the men lumbered over to us, closely followed by his armed cohorts. In the back seat, we were too fearful to move. Jeanette and I tightly held Mother's hands as she whispered in our ears not to be afraid.

"Cole," the leader said to Father in a deprecating way, "When did you and Tracy team up?"

Easy to anger, Father replied harshly, "My name is Bert Lacy, and who are you?"

"I'm the sheriff, and you still look like Cole to me."

Father reached into a hip pocket, pulled out his wallet, took out a business card and thrust it at the sheriff. "Here's my business card. I'm the advertising manager for the two Spokane newspapers, the Spokeman's Review and the Chronicle."

"If you're not Cole, why are you with Tracy? How long have you known him?"

"Isn't it obvious," Father replied sharply. "His car broke down and I'm giving him a ride to Priest River."

"You know who he is, don't you?"

"As far as I know, he's a business man in Newport."

"And Priest River and Spokane and Sandpoint and probably Coeur d'Alene and points in between. He's a bootlegger. And how do I know you're not in cahoots with him? You tried hard enough to get away."

"I was merely trying to avoid eating your dust."

"I'm going to have to go through your bags — make sure you're not making a bootleg run to Priest River."

Growing angrier with each insulting insinuation and each moment of delay, Father blurted out, "I'm a respected member of the First Presbyterian Church, a law abiding citizen, so be careful with your accusations. You can search our bags, but don't get anything dirty!"

The sheriff and his two men pawed through our bags, then ordered us out of the car and lifted the seats out and looked under them. They lifted the hood and peered into every nook and cranny, thrust their hands into the darkened recesses. They peered under the car, under the fenders, but couldn't find a single bottle.

"Okay," the sheriff said. "You're clean. I ought to run you in for reckless driving. If it weren't for your family, I would." Then the three stormed over to their car leaving the mess for us to straighten out. I watched as they sped off toward Newport.

Standing quietly off to the side until this moment, Tracy came over to Father and said, "I suppose you won't want me to ride with you any farther."

Still angered, Father shot a furrowed look at Tracy, staring hard and long. He seemed torn by his loathing for the sheriff, and his principles of right and wrong, the red neck insensitive bullying of the sheriff and the act of bootlegging. Finally his face softening he said gently, "We're wasting time. Get in the car."

Tracy, showing humiliation, took his place in the front seat. We sat quietly for a long time, pondering the explosive recent events.

But slowly the gloom lifted. Mother and Aunt Grace resumed their chattering. Father and Tracy forgetting the difference in their principles were soon submerged in light-hearted banter, enumerating the details of the great race. They laughed over the prospect of sharing a cell in the county jail — the one for bootlegging, the other for racing with the county sheriff. Sister Jeanette and I laughed with them, not quite knowing why.

Then Tracy, in rising good humor, reached into the inside pocket of his suit coat and pulled out a half-pint silver flask, and said, "They couldn't search my person, or I'd have been in trouble."

Turning to Father he offered, "Care for a drink?"

"No thanks," Father declined. Then making clear his moral stand added, "I don't drink."

Tracy extended the flask to Mother and Aunt Grace, and asked if they'd care for a drink. Both demurely declined, Mother showing shock and Aunt Grace a trace of pleasure at being offered a drink by a man, an attractive roguish man.

Tracy then turned back to Father and asked, "Would you mind if I had a drink?"

"No, it's your choice. But remember the children," he added, lowering his voice.

Tracy took a quick appreciative swallow and returned the flask to his pocket. He and Father continued talking, both enjoying each other's company; Father obviously liked this Robinhood who so boldly challenged the authorities. Suddenly, Tracy erupted in laughter. Father asked, "What's so funny?"

"The sheriff, thinking you were Cole." Then taking a long look at Father, he said, "You know there is a resemblance — your high forehead, your gray eyes, your ruddy complexion."

Father chuckled at the thought, enjoying a moment of wickedness. And then he asked in growing curiosity, "What was that all about, back there?"

"Oh, when I returned to my apartment early this morning, I found that it had been ransacked. The sheriff, I'm sure, was hoping to catch me with a stash of Canadian whiskey. It comes down the trails above upper Priest Lake, by mule string or backpack, at night. I sell only the best. Brings the top prices and profits.

"When I found that my apartment had been broken into, I knew it was getting too hot for me in Newport and time to move the operation to my headquarters in Priest River. Idaho's wide open, little chance of being bothered there. But the big money's made in Washington, in Spokane. As soon as things cool down — three, four months — I'll move back. But not Newport. Dishman, Chatteroy, or Opportunity — nearer Spokane."

"Sounds like a risky business to me," Father said.

"Not really. I hop back and forth across the border. Keep a step ahead of the law. Sorry you were involved."

We were approaching the point in the road where it would plunge down to the Pend Oreille River, a hill so steep it reminded me of the first drop of the amusement park roller coaster. It quickened the pulse, put butterflies in the stomach, because at the bottom there was a sharp turn to the right. Several car's brakes had failed on this hill over the years, and the cars with their passengers plunged into the river. Like a nightmare, images of our brakes failing, Father slicing into the earth embankments, throwing the car into reverse, the gears burning out, the car out of control flashed through my mind.

Involuntarily my feet pressed hard against the floor. I closed my eyes to the awesome sight. And then I felt the car plunge down the hill, slow at the bottom, sweep around the steeply banked curve at the bottom, on to an iron bridge, and strum across its corrugated metal floor.

I opened my eyes to Main Street, Priest River, its boardwalks stretching down each side. The walks were lined with lumberjacks, miners and itinerant workers who had bedrolls containing all their earthly goods suspended from their shoulders with rope. Every other building held a bar or bawdy house (Mother called them houses of ill repute), or both that catered to these rough men.

Tracy asked to be let out at a gaudy, red two-story building with shiny brass door plate and fittings and red velvet drapes billowing out the open windows of its second floor. As he stepped from the car, he reached into a side pocket of his trousers and pulled out a fat roll of bills, peeled off a twenty and offered it to father. "For the ride and your trouble," he said.

"Thanks, but it's not necessary," Father declined. A twenty-dollar bill then was a sound twenty dollars and important money, but I suppose Father wished to keep things on a friendly basis and not dishonor his convictions with hypocrisy.

Tracy then asked if he couldn't give the boy and girl each a silver dollar, "For soda pop, candy and perhaps a movie."

Father nodded his approval, and we eagerly stretched out our hands to accept the shiny silver dollars, envisioning all the things they'd buy. Tracy turned and strolled through the door of the red-fronted building. We never saw Tracy again. I've wondered if the red-fronted building was his Priest River headquarters. I've often wondered, too, if he were ever caught.

JIM LOW

IT WAS 1923. PRIEST LAKE WAS FAR FROM THE OUTSIDE WORLD, A pristine wilderness, and time was turned back to the 19th century. It was a land still basking in the sunshine of another era where travel was limited to foot or boat.

The West Branch Road was not yet connected to Luby Bay, so the only access to Priest Lake was the East Branch Road from Priest River. It was a stone-studded, often muddy track laced with corduroy, that brought you to Coolin, a tiny village at the south end of the lake, where you boarded a steamer that delivered you to Luby Bay.

There were only four families and four cabins on the bay at the time. To the west of the cabins on a rise of land was Jim Low's homestead. His one-room log cabin looked out over a clearing he had cut from the forest and on to Priest Lake and the Selkirk Mountains beyond.

Luby Bay was a veritable paradise for children. There was little trouble to get into, and we were allowed to roam much at our own whim. When we were not swimming, hiking, building sand castles or looking for arrowheads at the Indian Camping Grounds, we would walk up to Jim's homestead. We were fond of him and he of us, and our affection grew as the years passed.

Then families came to Luby Bay for the summer, the fathers only on weekends and vacations. Life was simple, unhurried. It was peaceful, the solitude broken only by the scolding of a Steller's jay or red squirrel. A motor boat coming into the bay was a rare sight, and all came down to the beach to see who the visitor could be. Life revolved around the white, sandy beach; sunning and swimming during the day and bonfires and roasting of marshmallows at night. Jim would see the light from the bonfires and come down.

I often stole alone up to see Jim, to hear him talk about his early times, and watch him while he worked. One time I found him in his barn seated on a three-legged stool milking his cow, skillfully directing stream after stream of milk into a galvanized steel pail. I had never witnessed the operation and watched in wide-eyed astonishment. I was six years old.

"Ever do much milking?" he asked.

"Never," I admitted.

"Well, I guess now's as good a time as any to learn," he said. "Sit down on the stool."

I did, which put me at eye level with the big, white four-fingered bag hung on the under side of the animal.

"Now take hold of one of the teats."

I did. It felt rough and hard and rubbery, and I wanted to drop the abominable thing, but with Jim standing over me I felt compelled to hang on.

"Now what you do is squeeze and pull down at the same time."

I squeezed and pulled and a white stream shot into the milk pail.

"Good," he said. "Now take hold of another teat. First pull down on one and then the other, and you double your production."

I did and kept a steady stream pouring into the milk pail.

"OK. You can stop now. Next what you need to know is the anatomy of a cow. You see that front left teat?"

"Yes."

"That one gives plain milk. That one beside it cream. The back left one coffee cream, and back right whipping cream."

"Jeepers! What about chocolate milk," I asked playing right into his hands.

"This is a Jersey cow. You need a Guernsey for chocolate milk," he asserted.

The barn was set in a little ravine beside his cabin. There the earth was black, rich, and there he had a vegetable garden. Alongside the barn was a watering trough he had hollowed out of a large cedar log. A cast-iron pipe brought fresh flowing water to it from a spring.

When Jim sold the cow, he hewed a point at one end of the log with his double-bitted ax and made it into a dugout canoe. He also hewed two paddles. He gave me the canoe and paddles.

Though now a canoe, it had the memory of a log, rolled like a log, and consequently was a challenge to keep upright. The ultimate challenge was to stand in it and birl it like a lumberjack. I learned how to do this from Jim who often came down to our beach to swim and paddle about in the canoe with me. I had the canoe for several years. Then one summer when we came out to the lake it was gone from where we left it high on the beach above the normal spring high water level. Gone. Stolen.

Jim was different from the other homesteaders. Where many gave up and left the country, he saw opportunity and persevered. Where they were withdrawn and didn't talk about their past, he was outgoing and talked freely about himself. He came from a pioneering family of twelve children. Four died in childhood.

His father worked in logging camps. They moved wherever his work took him; Wild Rose Prairie, Baileys Lake, Camden, Echo, Wrenco and Colville. They moved by wagon, a wagon equipped with a wood cook stove giving them a traveling kitchen. Each had his place to sleep under the wagon.

The death of his stepbrother Harry, a cripple from polio, still weighed heavily upon him. He spoke of getting Harry out in the sun on warm days. Harry made railroads and dump trucks from scraps of wood with which they played. One evening they had a wonderful time playing with a steam engine an uncle had given them. The next morning they found that Harry had died during the night. A neighbor came in and helped lay Harry out. They buried him in a homemade coffin in a small cemetery a few miles out of Camden. Later he came back to visit Harry's grave, but the graveyard had become overgrown, and he couldn't find the grave in the tall grass.

He spoke of one room schoolhouses, of train wrecks he'd seen, of a strawberry roan pony his father gave him, and his first job as a bootblack in Camden. When he was old enough, he worked in logging camps and sawmills, on trail crews, as a smoke chaser, and as a lookout for the Forest Service. He spoke of being in the war, World War I, and of a buddy who had been gassed.

Jim made trolling rigs for Father and me and taught us how to troll for the cutthroat trout that lay at the drop-off along the bay. And later, when we had graduated to fly rods, he took us into beaver ponds in the backcountry that yielded big, beautiful cutthroat trout. He showed us where the best huckleberry patches were. One Sunday he stopped at our cabin, took Father aside, and said he had a deer hanging in his barn and wouldn't we like a roast. Though it was out of season, Father quickly overcame any moral reservations that arose and said yes, we would. Mother served the roast for Sunday dinner.

The day he brought the white-faced pony was a dream come true. It was a wish I often expressed. "For you," he said, "for the summer."

And then, "You'll have to take good care of him, Tommy. Feed him. See that he has water. Curry him. He's from my father's homestead."

Jim showed me how to saddle him and ride, but best of all I liked to ride him bareback, barefooted, gallop free as the wind. It was a new found freedom, my horizons widened. I could fish far off places. It was the wondrous summer of my tenth year.

Life dealt Jim a rather poor hand, but he played his cards right and parlayed a one-room schoolhouse education and a magical personality into a tidy fortune. He built on each job that came along and saved his money. He once dug a trench three feet deep and 2,000 feet long through sand and gravel and roots and logs to bring running water to the bayside cottages. He did it all by hand, alone, with shovel, ax and crosscut saw. For this he was paid $300.

In the summer of 1924, he opened Low's Resort on three 150-foot government leased lots at the south end of Luby Bay. He built a small log cabin for himself and four rental cabins. He roofed them with cedar shakes. The interiors were spartan, the furniture hewed from logs, few cooking utensils, oil lamps and a privy in back. But people came to bask in the warmth of Jim's friendship, and they returned year after year.

Jim married a lady named Myrtle and had three children. The

resort grew, yet Jim chafed under the federal restrictions of the lease program. When the Forest Service offered a parcel of land at The Narrows south of Granite Creek, Jim put a bid on it.

It was a lovely strip of land with 1,800 feet of beach front, a white, sandy point and a fabulous view of Chimney Rock and the Selkirk Mountains. Jim offered $450. It was the only bid. Ridiculously low, but the Forest Service accepted it with $45 down and ten years to pay the balance. By 1960, beachfront lots were selling for $150 a front foot.

Jim built a lodge and fourteen log cabins. And where a narrow slough entered the lake, he dug a channel and erected a shed over it for boat storage.

For several years, I saw Jim infrequently. He visited me and my family in Ann Arbor, Mich., shortly before he died in February of 1971. The doorbell rang and there he was in navy overcoat, gray-striped suit, polished black shoes and crisp felt hat — a far cry from the faded blue jeans, blue workshirt, crumpled felt hat and worn White boots I remembered. My boys hung on his every word as I had so many years ago. He told them stories of Priest Lake. I offered him a drink, and he said, "Yes, a shot glass of bourbon with a water chaser, Tommy."

Chapter 5

COLONEL TUCKER'S SON

IT WAS A LIE AND NOT TO BE CONDONED, OF COURSE, YET IT showed a certain creativity and elan quite commendable in a boy of fourteen.

You see it all had begun when my gentle, little mother had said, "I'd rather you didn't hike all alone to Hunt Peak. You are only fourteen, Tom. There are grizzly bears up there and dangerous cliffs. And there is no longer a fireguard at the Hunt Peak Lookout should you run into trouble."

She was right. It was dangerous. There were cliffs and grizzly bears, yet how could I resist such a tantalizing description? Certainly no more than I could resist her description of Hangman Creek.

"You must promise me you will never, ever swim in Hangman Creek. There are dangerous undercurrents, and quicksand and hidden ledges."

My pal, Charles MacKenzie Kroll, and I swam in Hangman Creek for a number of years and found it to be everything Mother said it was — dangerous, deliciously dangerous and most enjoyable.

So there it was the summer of 1932. I, wondering how I might slip Mother's gentle restraints and she, wondering how she might keep her elusive son from slipping off to Hunt Peak.

She had had ample evidence of my special talents only the past winter when she had decided that if she were ever to make a gentleman of me, a wish she often expressed, it was time I learned some of the social graces and promptly enrolled me in dancing classes.

Hearing of this, Mrs. Kroll decided that Charles, too, was lacking in social graces and enrolled him in dancing classes. So each Friday night we dutifully attended dancing and social graces classes at a dance studio in downtown Spokane.

We learned how to ask a young lady to dance, whirl her gracefully across the dance floor, return her to her seat in the long row of chairs and, bowing, thank her for the dance. We endured three sessions and then opted for the double feature Western movies at the Granada Theater adjacent to the dance studio.

Miss Penrose, a maiden lady, finally inquired about our absences, and our mothers decided that we were as socially graceful as we could ever be and abandoned the project.

Hunt Peak was one of the higher peaks in the Selkirk Mountain Range that ran along the east shore of Priest Lake and on into Canada. It lay directly across Priest Lake from our cabin on Luby Bay. There was then a Forest Service trail from the east shore to Hunt Peak. The trail was nine miles long and rose 5,000 vertical feet.

In the summer of 1932, northern Idaho was still a remote, wild country. There were a few summer people, Forest Service employees, prospectors, lumberjacks and sourdoughs at isolated spots around Priest Lake, and a few homesteaders along the dusty, two-lane county road that was our only link to the village of Priest River thirty miles to the south.

Electricity was still many years off. We lived as Mother had when she was young; reading by kerosene and gasoline lamps, pumping water from a hand pump, cooking over a wood burning cast-iron stove, ironing with old cast irons that were heated on the back of the stove. It took Mother back to a time she loved.

Jim Ward, who was stationed at Luby Bay at the time, laid out the trail to Hunt Peak when he had been district ranger in the Kaniksu National Forest some years earlier. He was proud of the low gradient he had been able to maintain from top to bottom. And that was the way he had laid it out, starting at Hunt Peak and working down.

He was one of the early ones, and I liked to hang around when he was on the beach or out by his woodshed. In the quiet wistful tones of a man who could never hike the mountain crests again, he talked of the alpine meadows, the alpine lakes, the mountain goats and grizzly bears that inhabited the Selkirk Crest, and the endless mountain ranges that disappeared into Canada to the north, Montana to the east and Washington to the west.

Often after being with him, I would slip down to our warm sandy beach with my old brass bound telescope, lie propped against a driftwood log and scan the granite-capped Hunt Peak and ridge for a glimpse of one of Jim Ward's mountain goats and dream of hiking his trail.

The Selkirks, a range of glacial-carved mountains flanked by pine- and fir-clad ridges, were particularly beautiful in the evening, and I would watch their colors change from dark green, to smoky blue, to lavender and finally black. Often at night when we would sit by our beach bonfires, storms would come in over the range, and we would watch the lightning dance along the highest peaks and ridges.

At this time, the Civilian Conservation Corps (CCC) were working in Luby Bay. They were removing underbrush and fallen trees and improving the trail that skirted the shoreline. I became friends with one of the boys. Mother liked him and had him over for dinner one evening. We had small Eastern brook trout I had caught, oven-baked french fries, stewed tomatoes and tart Western huckleberry pie with a dollop of ice cream from the Colbert Ranch. A few days later he invited me to come to dinner at the CCC camp at Kalispel Bay a few miles to the north of us, and Mother said I could go.

The Kalispel Bay CCC Camp was run along military lines. The commanding officer was a Colonel Tucker. There was a parade grounds and the American flag was still flying when I arrived at camp. There were a number of unpainted barracks in which the boys lived. I was immediately hustled into one by my friend. The interior was early army. There were two rows of iron cots covered with government issue blankets. Over the head of each cot was a shelf on which the boys kept their personal possessions. There were no curtains at the windows. The floors were bare pine bleached from daily scrubbings.

My friend informed me that guests were not permitted for dinner and that I would have to wear some of his clothes. The shirt and pants were scratchy wool, olive-drab issue and fit fairly well, but I sloshed around in his hightopped shoes.

After I had dressed, we went out on the parade grounds for a game of softball. Promptly at 6 p.m. we were assembled for the nightly flag ceremony. I was concealed at center rear rank and escaped detection. The flag was lowered, properly folded, and we filed into the mess hall for dinner.

Dinner was a beef stew, fresh baked bread and jam, bug juice, pears and a dry crumbly frosted white loaf cake. It was typical, unimaginative army mess, yet the boys ate quickly like puppies, fearful there might not be enough. They came from homes where dinner was not always a sure thing.

After dinner, we played more softball. And then it was time for me to leave so that I would not be on the trail after dark. I changed my clothes, thanked my friend and hit the trail.

It was on the way back to the cabin that the splendid inspiration came to me. I would tell Mother that I had met Colonel Tucker's son and that he wanted to hike to Hunt Peak with me. She wouldn't know the colonel did not have a son, so no harm could be done.

I would, however, have to be very careful in answering Mother's cross examination which would surely follow my announcement of his existence and interest in hiking. I decided on an upbeat, positive approach hoping to override any questions or doubts my mother's natural instincts might raise.

When I arrived at the cabin, I could see the gas lantern burning brightly on the card table through the French doors of the living room and Mother, Grandma and sister Jeanette playing flinch.

Good!

They would be waiting for me to be the fourth for bridge, and if anxious enough the interrogation would be brief.

But first a word about Grandma and flinch. Grandma, a peppery, skimpy woman with a beehive hairdo reinforced with a switch, was a Victorian Presbyterian. She had set the ground rules for sister Jeanette's and my religious upbringing which included Sunday school and church each Sunday, Christian Endeavor, all church dinners and no cards on Sunday.

I once asked Grandma, "Why can't we play bridge on Sundays?"

And she had answered, "Because you can gamble with bridge, and gambling is forbidden by the Scriptures."

Grandma was up on that sort of thing, because every afternoon she would retire to her bedroom for an hour or two to rest and read her Bible. Though flinch was played with cards, Grandma decreed that you cannot gamble with flinch, so on Sunday evenings flinch was in and bridge was out. I could never comprehend the subtle difference, but I didn't argue with Grandma. At least we had flinch. I think it was Grandma's "Hangman Creek."

I burst into the living room with my good news and was pleasantly surprised with the response.

"How nice," Mother said, "a colonel's son?"

"Yes, the colonel's only son," I white-lied.

"When would you two be going?" she asked, obviously favorably impressed with the boy's status.

"Day after tomorrow," I replied. Any delay would only offer opportunity for discovery of my deception. "Can I go?"

"How old is he?" she asked.

"Fifteen," I replied. "He's big and strong for his age."

"You may go, but do be careful and stay together," she admonished.

The next day I made preparations for the hike — laid out my boots, heavy wool socks, Levi's, wool shirt and sweater. I would be leaving around 5 a.m., and mountain mornings could be quite chilly even in August. Later in the day, when it warmed, I would tie the sweater around my hips. My lunch — two PB&J sandwiches, orange, ice box cookies and two Hershey Bars — went into a used sugar sack which I would tie to my belt leaving my hands free. Grandma had been so delighted that I would be going with such a nice boy that she bought the Hershey Bars. She, too, had been favorably impressed with the colonel's-son ploy.

I went to bed early that night, first setting the Big Ben wind up alarm clock for 5 a.m. Mother came out on the porch as usual, tucked me in and kissed me goodnight. I had a twitch of conscience but not sufficient to call off the hike. I burrowed down in my blankets and went to sleep with the sound of waves, a nightly phenomena, lapping on the beach.

I awoke a few minutes before 5 o'clock and thought I would slip away quietly, but Mother came out of her bedroom shortly and made my breakfast. Again I felt the twitch of conscience but nothing serious.

The sun was just clearing the Selkirks and washing the highest peaks with orange light when I gathered my gear, walked down to our cedar pole floating dock and shoved off in our old boat, the Mary. She was powered by a four-horsepower Elto outboard motor that had a fly wheel and crank knob on top. With a few turns, it came to life, and I was putt, putting up the bay.

I headed towards Kalispel Bay, passed Indian Camp Grounds and disappeared around the point. The lake was smooth here and except for an osprey sailing down bay, I was the only living thing stirring. I went as far as the CCC camp allowing Mother ample time to get back in bed and then struck out boldly across Kalispel Bay, hugged the south side of Kalispel Island and out into the open waters of Priest Lake.

Here the waters were running fairly high, but the Mary just rolled over the waves. With her oak frame, rounded sides and flat bottom, she could take the worst storms that Priest Lake could throw at her.

If you can love a boat, I loved the Mary. She was my swimming companion, my fishing partner, my confidante, my friend, my refuge from three overprotective females.

Priest Lake is six miles wide here, and it took me an hour to make the crossing to the east shore where Hunt Creek comes in. I pulled the Mary well up on shore so that waves could not float her away.

Seeing Hunt Creek reminded me how much Mother liked dipping white fish there in the fall of the year. It was an art, done at night in the swift stream with a long-handled dip net in one hand and a lantern fashioned from a coffee can and candle in the other. With practice, you could dip five or six fish with one scoop. Mother would be so excited when she and Father would return with an apple box full of silvery fish that appeared to have been stamped out by machine in thirteen inch lengths. It was probably mother's only vice, because, you see, it was illegal and dodging the game warden was what made it so sporty. When they legalized dipping white fish with a limit of fifty fish, my gentle mother and father never dipped white fish again.

I looked about and soon found Jim Ward's trail. It was flat, damp in the early going along Hunt Creek, but soon rose abruptly up a flight of switchbacks then angled up the north slope of the Hunt Creek Valley. The trail was worn deep by the hoofs of pack-trains. It occasionally broke out of the dry ponderosa pine forest onto grassy patches and points where I could see ahead to the crest of the Selkirks and Hunt Peak and Gunsight Peak. In the clear air they seemed near, but I knew the falseness of their promise.

I was walking easily and happily. Though I enjoyed hiking with friends and family to lesser peaks, this was the best: To be alone and not feel the least lonely; to smell and feel and see things more keenly; smell the potpourri fragrance of live and dead needles of pine and fir and spruce and cedar; feel the hot sun that raised a sweat and the cool of the breeze that blew through my wool shirt; see the red splashes of Indian paintbrush, the pink princess pine, the pale blue harebell and the red fruited kinnikinnick.

Shortly the trail dipped into the valley of the north fork of Hunt Creek. Here were giant cedars and little light filtered through. It was cool and the forest floor was covered with dark green moss.

Jim Ward's trail soon divided. The left fork continued up to a lookout on Horton Ridge. The right fork, which I took, crossed Hunt Creek on a log bridge and zigzagged upwards to the top of a ridge that separates the north and south forks of Hunt Creek.

I had been hiking steadily, and had to take a slower pace and an occasional "five" to negotiate the lengthy series of switchbacks. I finally reached the ridge top. The trail turned up its southern slope, into an open forest of lodgepole pine. I stopped from to time to drink from the streamlets that crossed my path. They were icy cold and varied in taste depending, I presume, on the minerals in them. The elevation was around 6,000 feet, and the slopes were accented with yucca-like bear grass with its coarse bunches of grass-like leaves at the base and two to three foot woody stalks topped by a white snowball flower.

I came upon a great huckleberry patch that at this elevation still bore berries though it was well past the season in the lower elevations. I was a bit apprehensive, because it was here that Jim Ward had said I might run into grizzly bears feeding on the berries. He had once been treed by a grizzly sow with two cubs on this stretch of trail.

I worried about having to climb one of the slender lodgepole pines and whether I would be quick enough to avoid a raging grizzly sow's rush. So I was quite relieved when I emerged from the huckleberry patch into a more open, grassy, park-like terrain sparsely forested with whitebark pine and alpine fir.

Of all the trees, alpine fir is my favorite. It must be nature's, too, because she uses this dark green, spire-like tree to accent a meadow's edge, a ridgetop, a river's bend. It is a tree of wild, free spaces, not one to end as a captive on city lawns.

Soon I reached the headwall below Hunt Peak and the trail took an abrupt right turn. It led upwards through a dense bed of salal bushes whose shiny, dark green, leathery leaves gave off a pungent odor that made my nose tingle. The air became thin, my breathing quickened, and I had to take a "five" from time to time. Once when I stopped, I was startled by the thunderous take-off of several great blue grouse and watched as they set their wings and glided to a ridge far down the mountainside.

As I climbed farther, the salal gave way to gray granite interspersed with dwarf whitebark pine. They were old, yet no more than six feet tall. And then abruptly I emerged on the bare crest of the Selkirk range. As I walked up to the lookout building, I noticed that it was anchored to the granite surface with thick guy wires and that just beyond was a great void.

I crawled forward and peered over the edge. There was a sheer drop of a thousand feet, and in a cirque to my left was a small turquoise blue alpine lake. To my right in another cirque was a lake colored red from algae just as Jim Ward had described it all to me.

I immediately fell in love with this incredibly beautiful alpine country. Dwarfed and gnarled whitebark pine, now no more than two to three feet high, sprouted out of cracks in the granite and little depressions of decayed rock. There were little alpine meadows edged with alpine fir beyond the lakes, and in sheltered nooks, melting snowbanks nourished tardy spring flowers. To the north, I could see the sculpted peaks of the Selkirks — Chimney Rock, Goblin's Nob, Lion Head, Hay Stack, Lookout Mountain, Molly's Nipple, Phoebe's Tit and, finally, Snowy Top at the Canadian border. Those robust, early-day names have given way to "Phoebe's Tip" and "Molly's."

It was a vast primordial country, free, silent, wild. There was a haunting, mystical feeling to it. Perhaps the same feeling the Indian shamans experienced when they climbed the mountain peaks for inspiration for their visions.

I found a flat topped boulder to sit on and removed the lunch sack from my belt. It was well past noon. As I ate, I looked for the band of mountain goats that used the area, but none were visible. An occasional hawk soared past and rock coneys hurried about among the boulders busy with their haying operation. When I came to the Hershey Bar for Colonel Tucker's son, I laughed out loud and startled the coneys. It had been so easy. Now I could hike wherever I wanted the rest of the summer with the colonel's only son.

After lunch, I once again crawled to the edge of the over-hanging rock face and pushed a stone over. My stomach went with it as I watched it fall and then bound in great leaps across the cirque floor. I spit so I could say later that I had spit a thousand feet.

Tiring of this, I took a walk along the ridge that extended to the north from Hunt Peak. I looked into ravines and sheltered basins hoping to see mountain goats bedded down. I did see signs on the ground, but the goats eluded me, and I was disappointed.

When I returned from my walk, I entered the lookout building. It was of typical Forest Service design; approximately fifteen feet square, with windows on all four sides that were shuttered. The interior was bare. The firefinder, the stove, the fold-away iron cot, the crank telephone, the usual stock of pulp magazines had all been removed.

Jim Ward had said that the building had been left for hunters and hikers caught overnight on the mountain. A few years later, I was to man such a lookout in the Lolo Ranger District southwest of Missoula, Mont., during the summers that I was a college student.

At last it was time to leave if I were to reach the lakeshore before dark. The hike down took much less time, as I ran much of the way and took short cuts down the switchbacks. I found, that running downhill, I could take great leaps, and it was fun to jump logs that lay across the trail. When I arrived at the lake, the Mary was still high and dry, and I soon had her in the water and headed home. This time I circled out of sight around the north side of Kalispel Island, past Indian Picture Rocks, through Kalispel Bay and rounded the point at Indian Camp Grounds as though I were coming from the CCC camp.

It was dark and kerosene and gasoline lamps flickered in the cabins along the bay. The beaches were deserted, and it was quiet. There was a lone figure on our dock which I assumed to be Mother, but as I pulled in I could see it was sister Jeanette. It should have been Mother, and I had an uneasy feeling that something was very wrong.

"Mother stayed up after you left and saw you scoot past Kalispel Island," sister said. "She has been worried sick all day that something would happen to you. It was a terrible thing for you to do."

She whirled and ran up to the cottage. This was the same person who had written my excuses when I played hooky and always stood up for me in past emergencies. And now I was left alone to face Mother.

I tied the Mary up to the dock and approached the cabin with apprehension, wondering what my punishment would be. When I entered, Mother, Jeanette and Grandma were playing flinch. Mother's eyes were red, and she would not speak to me. It was the ultimate punishment.

She had kept my dinner in the warming oven of the stove. I ate in the kitchen alone and slipped quietly off to bed.

Mother did not speak to me for several days. The sentence was far heavier than had I been confined to quarters, the usual punishment. I did not feel in the mood for swimming, nor the evening fly fishing with the Mary along Woodrat Mine Point, nor reading pulp magazines with friend Ed in our hideaway over Schneider's ice house. I avoided Jim Ward. Then one night Mother came out on the porch and tucked me in bed and kissed me good night.

It was over.

Some things had changed. Some things had ended. In later years, Colonel Tucker's son became a legend, and some parts of Jim Ward's trail became a logging road and some parts just disappeared.

Chapter 6

DINTY MURPHY

DINTY MURPHY HAD COME INTO AND LEFT THIS WORLD WITH scarcely a ripple. He was a man alone, like so many of the time, with neither roots nor family.

At his funeral, there had been no great accomplishments that Father O'Brien could name with pride. Little he could say but that Dinty had come from County Cork, Ireland as a lad at the turn of the century; his mother and father gone with the tuberculosis, his brothers and sisters scattered and their scab of land too poor to hold him.

Father O'Brien did mention Dinty's contribution to the development of the Kaniksu as one of the early settlers, as a homesteader and lumberman (lumberjack). And he made romantic reference to his being one of the last of the sourdoughs and an avid outdoor sportsman (poacher).

But the standard words — sober, devoted family man — that

clergymen of the time often fell back on could not be used in Dinty's case. For Dinty was neither family man nor always sober. He often got pleasantly drunk at Belle La Fleur's bar.

And it was at Belle's that the services were held. Belle had cleared the bar room of tables and lined the chairs in neat rows as she did for the holy rites of mass each Sunday. Father O'Brien had used the bar as an altar for the services. And two of Belle's girls, whom she had brought over with her from Virginia City where she had been a madam, sang "When Irish Eyes are Smiling" and "Irish Lullaby," two of Dinty's favorite songs.

After the services, the tables were returned to their normal positions and the bar opened for a wake for Dinty. There had been hardly money enough in Dinty's faded Levi's to pay for one round of drinks, so Belle ordered, "Drinks on the house — for Dinty. All you can drink, boys."

And well she should have. Even then she probably put the tab on Archibald's account or rolled the boys afterwards.

But the boys never complained about her small trespasses. Archibald was sweet on Belle, and if his bill was high he never objected. If a lumberjack's roll disappeared overnight, the jack considered it money well spent. And as for Dinty, Belle and the girls were family, the only feminine company he knew.

When Dinty had first come to this country from Ireland, he had stopped for a brief time in New York City where he worked in an office. He never mentioned what the business was, but I know that the stay was brief because Dinty said, "If I'd stayed long in New York I'd be dead. We were like cattle shut up in a barn with no daylight, no fresh breezes and only four walls to look at."

From New York, Dinty had taken the Settlers Train to Priest River, Idaho. "When I got off the train, Tammy, I could see the tall mountains all about me reachin' to the sky, and I could fill my lungs with the sweet smell of the pine and cedar carried on the breezes." Dinty spoke with an Irish brogue; rolled his Rs and called me Tammy, not Tommy. He had a shovel chin, and when he spoke his lower lip curled over his lower teeth and the words seemed to be coming out over a mouthful of mush.

"Priest River couldn't have been much of a town then, Dinty. Weren't you concerned about getting some kind of work?"

"No! It was small but bustlin'. Jacks up and down Main Street, and every other building a bar. A high whine comin' from the lumber mill. I got a room in a small hotel. One day at a fine bar I struck up an acquaintance with a fellow named Archibald. He told me he was a homesteader. That his land lay twenty-six miles north in the grand Kaniksu Forest, surrounded by the glorious Selkirk Mountains, and but a mile west of Priest Lake, the most beautiful lake in all the world. I feasted on his words.

"And then when he said the land was free for the takin', all I had to do was prove up on it, meanin' clear a spot and build a house, I knew I'd been led to the right place."

"Like a dream," I said.

"That it was. Like a dream come true." he replied.

"The next day we took off up the West Branch Road, little more than a track through the great tall forest, his wagon loaded down with supplies. He'd been kind enough to tell me what I'd need and made room in the wagon for all of it. It was slow going what with the long stretches of corduroy and mud and chuck holes. Often we'd have to get out and push where the mud was deep and gummy and where the grade was steep. I don't know which was worse, bein' thrown about on the hard board seat or straining and pushin' that wagon. But what beautiful sights we saw; deer, mule deer by the score in the meadows and glens along the road. Archibald said, 'There are deer enough so no man need go hungry.'

"There was a beautiful falls that poured out of a rocky cleft in the low hill above the crossin' of the Lower West Branch. Archibald jumped out of the wagon and motioned for me to follow him up the rocky cleft. I clambered after him, and soon we broke out of the cleft and there was a little lake spread out before us. We'd crossed a rock dike. The water dropped straight off, so clear I could see long trout sweepin' about in the depths below me."

"I've seen it, but the new road cuts through the cleft and drained the lake," I said.

"Aye. It's a shame, Tammy. We made three more stream crossings in the afternoon; Upper West Branch, Binarch Creek and Lamb Creek. All the time, we were passin' through a forest of virgin white pine, fir and cedar. At times it was like goin' through a tunnel. It was a world of trees and streams and mountains, dark and at first overpowin', but then we'd break out into a viewpoint where we could see the jagged outline of the Selkirk Mountains far ahead, so beautiful they could charm you for a lifetime.

"It was near midnight when we arrived at Archibald's homestead, one of the finest in the great meadows along Lamb Creek and Reynolds Creek. The kind man invited me to stay the night and said we'd look over the available land in the morning.

"We were up at first light. Archibald hustled about fixin' a hearty breakfast of sourdough pancakes, thick slices of slab bacon and strong black coffee. He told me to go outside and have a look around while he got breakfast ready.

"You could see he was prosperous; the hay in the meadow freshly cut and stacked, cattle feedin' along the creek, his barn all tidy and his barbed wire fence pulled taut and sparklin' in the sun's early rays. But the view, the view was what took my fancy; the valleys of Lamb Creek and Reynolds Creek joined at the north end of his land. You could look up those two mountain rimmed valleys to the very edge of the world.

"Across the West Branch Road I noticed a small piece of meadow that looked unclaimed. I asked Archibald about it at breakfast.

" 'You've a fine eye for land,' Mr. Murphy, he said, giving me the title of mister and makin' me feel all important, me being but a lad and him bein' older. I was planning to call it to your attention. It's only an eighty acre parcel, but it has three more fine meadows on it and some valuable white pine and cedar. And, most important, it has free access to the West Branch Road.'

" 'The access thing, I do not understand,' I said, almost afraid to show Archibald my ignorance. But I needn't have worried.

"Archibald patiently explained, 'Access means you can reach your land without crossing over someone else's property.'

"And then he told me a story by way of explanation.

" 'The meadows are cut up into several small homesteads. There is Lemley's and Green's and others. Green's only access to the West Branch Road is over a corner of Lemley's land. Lemley warned him not to cross his property forcing Green to take a torturous round about route through the woods.

" 'Angered by Lemley's lack of Western hospitality, Green continued openly to cross over Lemley's land. So Lemley laid in wait for him to cross and when he did Lemley pulled down on him with a .30-.30 and killed him. The jury acquitted Lemley, trespassing being considered as serious an offense as wife stealing at the time.' "

"So that's how you happened to pick this particular piece of land, Dinty," I put in. He'd grown quiet, his eyes wandering away to that far off time. "I suppose you built your house and barn and added a few cows then," I added urging him on.

"I built my log barn and house, Tammy, but that took most of my money, and I had to take a job lumberjacking with the Dalkena Lumber Co. that was starting up logging in the area.

"I worked for wages for awhile, and then my partner and I gypoed."

"What's that, Dinty?" I asked.

"Gypoing is where you get paid for the number of board feet you cut in a day. My partner and I would start early and work late, hardly took time out for lunch. You could say we were on our own. And we earned a lot more money."

Logging was done mostly in the winter when the logs could be skidded easily on the snow. They were stored along stream banks or floated in water filled flumes to Priest Lake and held in great log booms until ice-out in the spring.

Then the booms were towed by tug boat to the outlet of the Priest River. Millions of board feet of timber were herded down the roaring river, deep with snow melt from drifts in the mountains.

The log drive was a treacherous, perilous, tension-filled business. Often the jacks gambled their lives against their skill on the logs. But coming off months of deadening drudgery felling timber and womenless nights, they were ready to gamble their lives for the thrill of riding bucking logs down a hell roaring torrent of water.

The experienced jacks like Dinty were in the boat crews. They could log hop and knew how to use a peavey to pick apart the log jams that held up the drive.

I asked Dinty, "Were you ever afraid riding the logs?"

And he said, "Tammy, every minute you're out on those logs you ride with fear in your stomach, the roar of the river in your ears like some demon, the logs twistin' and turnin' and buckin' and the rocks so big they stick up through the ragin' river, reachin' out for you.

"I suffered a fall once and thought sure I was a goner," he said with a grimace. "The logs so thick and me under them. There'd been an early morning mist that veiled my eyes. But with the drive underway, there was naught to do but keep at it. I'd hopped on a log with a fat belly and a wobbly roll. It threw me, and the logs wrung me out as I passed through."

"Like a washing machine wringer," I put in sympathetically.

"That it was. The weight of my boots and heavy clothes and my peavy pulled me to the very bottom. Then a powerful current slammed me back up against the logs overhead. I caught a feeble light comin' through an opening in the logs and forced my peavey through it, wigglin' it back and forth 'til there was room for me to slip through.

"The boat crew bulled their way through the carpet of logs over to me and pulled me into the boat. I couldn't help, that gone I was from the freezin' water and the massagin' I took from the logs. But I'd been able to hold onto my peavey. They cost the company money and a jack's life didn't."

Thrilling to the telling and in open envy, I'd said, "Maybe some day I can be a lumberjack and ride the logs."

"No, Tammy. You stick with the books and amount to something someday," Dinty replied.

The last river drive was in 1949, but as early as 1932 the Dalkena Company began bringing logs by truck to Luby Bay and dropping them into a log boom at the south end of the bay. I watched the jacks move about on the logs and soon was doing it myself.

The logs would roll as you danced across them. The smaller ones would dip and sway and threaten to dump you in and the logs crush you. But if you moved fast enough, you could race across before the logs sank under you, reach the larger steadier boom logs that were chained end-to-end forming a pen and then turn around and dance back to shore. It was dangerous, and I felt the fear in my stomach and the excitement that Dinty spoke of.

And I'd imagine I was one of the jacks riding the logs in a great river drive.

It wasn't until later that Dinty and I became fishing partners, when he was in his late fifties and I was entering my teens. He was beginning to show the effects of his years as a lumberjack and riding the river. His face was lined, his hair graying. He was a little stooped, thinner, and his legs were bent at the knees. He still wore the garb of the lumberjack; the faded blue workshirt, Levi's stagged at the tops of his caulked White boots, and a rumpled, black felt hat.

We always scheduled our fishing expeditions for early in the morning; departure time 5 a.m. at his shack. It was a simple one room abode with narrow porch across the front of it, Western style. There was a hand-crafted bench near the door on which he could be seen in the evening gazing out over his garden, catching any vagrant breeze.

The walls of the shack were a double course of rough-cut cedar boards with a course of tar paper between. Within was a small simple table, two straight chairs, benches and a double bed he had put together from peeled logs and a few boards. The bed had a layer of straw for a mattress and tangles of comforters on top.

There were two small windows, cloudy and unfettered with curtains. A wool, red-checked mackinaw, a spare pair of Levi's, and a blue workshirt hung from wooden pegs stuck in the wall. Behind the only door was a jug of what I took to be white lightning. Dinty always took a long swig before we left for fishing.

Deer antlers and grouse fans decorated the walls, and a large black bear hide lay on the floor beside his bed. A .30-.30 rifle rested on a gun rack made from deer hoofs. I dreamed of having a cabin like it of my own and living at Priest Lake. Thoughts of college, career, marriage were a long way off.

In one corner was a small black cast-iron stove. On it rested a coffee can of sourdough. Always the sourdough cans rested on the backs of the cast-iron stoves of these lone men; the staff of life for the men called "sourdoughs." They used it to make bread, pancakes, muffins and biscuits.

Dinty's cooking utensils were few and hung from nails. His metal enameled plates and cups rested on a single shelf. A wooden apple box nailed to the wall served as a cabinet for his food supplies.

He lived on vegetables from his garden, fish, venison, wild berries and mushrooms. His few cattle were a cash crop, not to be eaten but sold to buy clothes, staples, pay taxes and finance an occasional drinking spree with Belle and the girls.

The first time Dinty and I fished together we were walking up the Lamb Creek Road when we heard a car coming up behind us. Suddenly I realized I was all alone. After the car passed, Dinty appeared from the brush at the side of the road.

I asked, "What on earth did you do that for, Dinty?"

"Tammy," he replied, "I don't have a fishing license and I was afraid it might be the game warden."

Dinty's meager budget would not cover fishing nor hunting licenses. So he had become quite adept at avoiding the law — poaching as it were. Poaching, being a sin and like most sin highly exciting and enjoyable, added a dash of spice to our fishing trips.

The car having passed out of sight, we continued up the road finally turning off on an old logging road that would take us to a beaver pond he had discovered when he was logging in the area. The road wound up through the hills. Tall hemlock, pines, fir and cedar reached over the road. In the damp shady areas, rays of sunlight lit up the tall green ferns that covered the forest floor. In the open areas, huckleberry bushes grew. We would scoop up a handful of the tart berries as we walked along. Now and then Dinty would say he heard a deer crash off through the undercover, but my ears were not keen enough to catch the sound.

I was eager to get to the dam, and Dinty admonished, "Take it easy, Tammy. You can walk forever if you pace yourself. Walk slowly and steadily."

After an interminable time, the road topped out on a high ridge and then descended abruptly into a deep draw ending on a bench that overlooked the beaver pond. It was fed by a small stream, tiny in comparison to the size of the pond. A heavy antlered deer that had been feeding in the shallow grassy flats at the upper end of the pond splashed noisily off into the woods, and in so doing put two nervous mallards to flight.

It was evident the ancient pond had been there many years. It was quiet, hushed, and I felt the remoteness, the wildness. We made our way through a pungent, buck-brush covered embankment to the water's edge. Dinty hopped onto a gray weathered log that reached out into the water. I chose the dam to fish from; walked out on it, stepped on a moss covered hole and plunged in over my knee, nearly losing my balance and toppling into the pond. I righted myself and took up a position on a short log imbedded in the dam itself. The sunlight pouring into the valley revealed large ghostly shapes moving in the deep water below me. I hurriedly extended my telescoping metal rod and laced a worm from Dinty's garden onto my Indiana Spinner. I let it flutter down into the water.

A heavy Eastern brook trout, followed by several lesser trout, rose to meet it. The larger trout look it. I felt its weight and reared back recklessly in my excitement, and the great trout, diving at the same time, bent the stiff rod nearly double. The fish made a run for a sunken log, there to bury the hook in its underside and break free. I applied all the pressure I could short of breaking the rod, not giving a worry to the leader, it being of heavy gut capable of holding a runaway horse. The fish reversed directions, coming at me so fast, I couldn't recover line quickly enough to prevent him from gaining the cover of a log at my very feet. I reached out with my rod as far as I could trying for an angle to apply enough pressure to force him out into the open water. Slowly I pulled him out, shaking his head from side to head, and I feared he'd bend the hook and tear it out of his jaw. Then he resorted to thrashing, rolling runs across the surface of the pond. I turned him, and turned him, and turned him again, finally led him up to the dam, slid him out onto it, and pounced on him. I delivered a killing blow to the back of his head and stuffed him into my canvas creel, his tail hanging well over the end.

It was not sporting; it was inelegant, but it was the dawn of my fishing experience, more exciting, more thrilling than anything else since.

While I was fighting the big fish, I was aware that Dinty had caught a fish or two. He had but the first and second sections of an old bamboo fly rod, a few yards of black cotton line, and a snelled hook — no leader nor reel. I watched as he plopped a gob of worms off the end of his log perch and saw the buggy-whip rod bend slightly. No deft handling here. Dinty reared back horsing the trout up and out and pinning it to his chest. Then grasping it firmly in his left hand, he removed the hook gave the trout a tap against the butt of the rod and dropped it into a used flour sack. Dinty gave no quarter. He was fishing for his supper and perhaps an extra fish or two for the next day.

The thrashing of my fish having put the other trout to flight, I made my way across the dam and up into the grassy flats. The water there was a foot or two deep and winding through it was the old stream channel. There were deep holes in the bends and where logs lay across it. I eased near the channel, then waited a few minutes before fishing because I had telegraphed my presence ahead to the trout.

I saw Dinty moving up the flats on the opposite side of the channel, he too having put the fish down. Suddenly he whooped and dropped out of sight. He'd stepped into a deep trench the beaver had dug to float logs out of the forest. All I could see was his hat floating on the surface and then him come spluttering up under it.

I smothered a laugh and asked piously, "You OK, Dinty?"

"I'm all right, Tammy. Keep a sharp eye out for beaver trenches. They're the devil's own traps, tucked as they are amongst the grasses."

The water was still icy from the snow melt in the mountains, and I knew that Dinty was suffering, but the sun was now high and hot and would soon dry out his thin shirt and Levi's and warm him.

To fish the flats, you had to cast over the marsh grasses out into the open channel. You stood mired hip deep in muck and water, so you were fishing blind, not knowing what sunken logs or tangles of sticks you might be casting into. You fished by feel.

I made my first cast to the middle of the channel and immediately felt a strong tug. I struck hard and fast, wanting to hook him firmly, then led him quickly through a sparse avenue in the grasses, lifted him to my chest and pinned him to me with my hat. In rapid succession I caught two more chunky Eastern brook trout that were no match for the steel rod and gut leader.

In the meantime, Dinty had been fishing a bend above me where the current had cut a deep pool, and had caught enough for a couple of meals. He moved down to me and said, "Let's call it a day, Tammy. We have enough. Leave a few for next time."

We pulled out, clambered up the embankment. When we reached the dusty Lamb Creek Road it was hot and dry, near 90 degrees.

"I'd give anything for a cold drink," I said to Dinty.

"Up ahead there's a fine spring by the side of the road," he replied. "You didn't notice it coming in?"

"No," I admitted. "I hope it's not far."

"Won't be long now," he assured me and sure enough, just ahead and not more than three feet off the road, we came upon a tiny spring.

Some thoughtful soul had dug a shallow well, lined it with boards and run a metal pipe to it from which flowed clear cold sparkling water. There were a few water bugs skittering over the surface. Dinty picked a rusty can off a branch that hung over the well, filled it to overflowing, passed it to me saying, "It's the finest water in all the world."

I looked to make sure there were no water bugs on it and wondered about the sanitary condition of the can. However, I took a deep drink. It chilled my teeth. It was pure and clear with a touch of flavor of wild mint to it and the best water I ever tasted. We always stopped there when we returned from our fishing expeditions.

It was shortly after this first fishing expedition that I overheard Mother and Father talking about Dinty; his drinking bouts and Belle and the girls, women of ill repute as Mother put it. Mother said that Dinty might not be a good influence on me, might lead me astray and finally, "Bert, you better have a talk with Tommy."

Most of my knowledge of sex had come from friends. It was not always accurate and often slanted by well meaning parents. For example condoms were rubber things you had to use when you had sex with a girl or you might get her pregnant or, worse, catch syphilis and end up a blithering idiot. Whores were white slaves, and I felt sorry for them.

When Father asked me what I knew about sex, I said, "You mean wearing a safe when you make out, claps, whores, that sort of thing?"

And he said, "That's the general idea, but where did you pick up that language ... from Dinty?"

"No, from guys at school. All Dinty talks about is fishing and hunting. He doesn't talk much."

"You know he drinks, gets drunk," he said sternly. Father being a Presbyterian did not approve of drinking.

"I know that. But Dinty's my friend. He'd never do or say anything to harm me."

"You know that Dinty consorts with prostitutes?"

"Whores?"

"I wish you wouldn't use that word. Yes, uh whores."

"I've heard that. But Dinty never talks about it. Older people don't like to talk about sex."

"I guess you've got that right. This isn't easy for me you know."

"I figured that."

"Well, I'm not going to ask you not to fish with Dinty. Just don't let me hear of you going up to Belle's." And that was the first and last time we ever talked about sex.

Piqued with wonder, I asked on our next fishing expedition, "Dinty, do you consort with whores?"

"Well, Tammy," he said, "I don't know what you mean by consort, but yes I do see the girls at Belle's, especially Dawn. They're company. We have a few drinks. Laugh a lot. They're understanding. They tease me and, if people tease you, you know they like you.

"I'm not much of a catch, Tammy. I don't have a fine home, fine clothes, a car, money, not much to look at."

"You look OK to me," I hastened to assure him.

"Thanks, Tammy, but women don't warm up to me. They give me a nod, a brief greeting, never, 'How are you Mr. Murphy?' No woman ever took a fancy to me other than Dawn. She loves me and I love her, but she's afraid to leave the security of Belle's. People like us — Dawn and the girls and me — we have a need for each other. They're all I've got. Do you understand, Tammy?"

"I think so, Dinty. It's OK with me."

We fished together many times that summer. We fished the beaver dams on the Lamb Creek flats at Last Hope Ranch and Colbert's and Elmer Henchel's homesteads. The flats were choked with brush sprinkled with the gray-paper yellow jacket nests. When you stumbled into one, the angry stinging devils would take after you, and you'd find you could sprint through tangles of brush you could barely claw your way through coming in. But we always came back for the big black Eastern brook trout that lay behind the dams and in the pools strung out upstream.

We fished the great beaver pond on upper Binarch Creek. It was large enough to float a sizeable raft allowing us to get into bushy coves otherwise inaccessible. The fish in Binarch Creek were large cutthroat left over from the spring spawning run. And we fished Kalispel Creek and some of the beaver ponds tucked away on its little feeder creeks.

Our fishing partnership lasted but a few years. Then it came time for me to go to college and work summers to help with my college expenses. World War II came along and it was a number of years before I saw Dinty again.

From time to time, I heard that Belle was trying to get Dinty to sign over his homestead to her; something about his account getting out of hand. But there was no way of knowing if it was Dinty's drinking or Belle's padding his bill that caused the problem.

The next time I saw Dinty I was married and brought my wife, Harriet, to see Priest Lake. I stopped at Van's Corners for a can of cold beer on returning from fishing the Lamb Creek flats.

I felt a pair of clawed hands on the back of my neck. I turned and there was Dinty beaming happily up at me. He was so happy to see me his eyes glistened. He was then in his seventies and quite stooped with age and arthritis. But he could still handle a drink, and I bought him a couple. He would toss off a shot glass of whiskey and follow it with a sip of water.

He said he had heard that I was married and that he'd like to see my bride. I felt ashamed that I had not stopped to see him. Harriet and I did stop at his home one afternoon, and he exclaimed how beautiful she was and how much he enjoyed meeting her.

The next time I heard of Dinty, Belle had finally persuaded him to sign over his homestead to her. She was going to put him off his land, but Jim Low and some of the old homesteaders told her they'd run her out of the country if she did not let Dinty live out his life on his land. Dinty lived only another two years. Some said he died of a broken heart.

Chapter 7

THE STRAWBERRY MAN

IF YOU WERE TO DRIVE UP THE LAMB CREEK ROAD TODAY PAST THE second serpentine curve, you'd see a cleared hillside in the forest to your right with a small sculpted niche in its center. A few trees still stand around it, but there is no trace of the one room cabin nor the chopping block nor the stacked firewood that once rested on the level surface of the niche. The summer house that perched on top of the hill is gone, vanished. And the shake-sided barn that was set between the cabin and the road, that too is gone. Not a cedar shake nor a scrap of screen nor a window pane nor a strawberry plant is left to remind you that once someone carved out a home here in the great Kaniksu wilderness.

It is like a memorial without the words, and if there were words they'd be simple words like the man himself: "Elmer Henchel, homesteader. He loved this valley." Like the other lone men who came to the Kaniksu at the turn of the century he didn't talk about himself. Where they came from and why was a mystery. So there were rumors that these men were on the run; a sheriff in Abilene, a woman in Shreveport.

The living was easy then, and it trapped these men like the islands of the lotus eaters trapped Ulysses and his men. The land was free for the taking, and so were the gifts of deer and fish and berries and mushrooms and timber. They came and stayed a lifetime.

Elmer was a small man, slender, scarcely five feet tall. He had a ruddy pinched face, sandy hair and a gold-toothed grin. He wore a World War I campaign hat pinched to form four dimples, army breeches and army shoes. His speech was nasal, and he continuously said, "Yah, Yah, Oh Yah." So people came to call him "Oh Yah."

He built his cabin from logs of white pine that grew on his homestead and roofed it with shakes he cut out of billets of cedar that also grew on his land. He set his chopping block and stacked his wood conveniently close to his door for the snows of winter were often waist deep. He could often be seen on a summer evening sitting on the chopping block, his back against the stacked firewood looking out over his valley.

High on the hill above he built his one room summer house. The lower half he covered with shakes. The upper half he covered with screen to catch the evening breezes no matter from which direction they might come. On summer nights, when the heat of day still lay heavily on the lowland, he'd sleep up there. From here he could see up and down the Lamb Creek Valley, the points and islands of dark green alpine fir that extended out onto the brush covered valley floor, the silver waters of the great beaver dam that lay at the east edge of his land and beyond to the distant rugged Selkirk peaks.

Between his cabin and the road he built a barn. He framed the barn with pine poles and covered the whole with cedar shakes. Within he kept a vintage Model T touring car and an early Model T delivery truck. The latter had a single seat, scarcely wide enough for two, and a small wooden bed with raised sides behind. He replaced the "ooga-ooga" horn with an air horn that emitted an eerie wail.

Often when I had been fishing the big beaver dam and was trudging down the hot dusty Lamb Creek Road, I'd hear the wail of the air horn as he negotiated each turn of the road. Soon he'd catch up with me and call out, "Hop in Tommy. It's too hot to be walking." It could heat up to over a hundred degrees on the Lamb Creek flats, and I'd hop in, grateful to be out of the burning sun.

He'd invariably want to know how I had done, and I'd open my creel and display the Eastern brook trout that lay in a bed of ferns. I'd ask if he could use a few, a tribute to pay for fishing his beaver pond.

"Just a couple," he'd say. "The little ones." And then he'd tell me the small ones were the sweetest. He never objected to the number I took, the supply seeming to be limitless.

Once I came out of the brush flats wet to the shoulders and covered with mud. He asked, "What on earth happened to you?"

"I jumped out into the middle of a slough," I replied. "The water appeared to be only a foot deep, and I thought I'd avoid walking way around the end of it through the brush. Besides, there's a yellow jacket nest at that end, and they've taken after me before.

"Promptly sank into mud up to my armpits. I couldn't pull my legs out, and I couldn't reach a branch from the other side to pull myself out. I thought I was a goner. I kept wiggling and squirming until, by leaning forward with my face in the water, I could just reach a tough old tag alder and slowly worked my way out."

"Tommy, you can't take chances when you're out there alone like that. Stay on the beaver dam itself and you can catch all the fish you need." And then he added, "Look carefully before you leap." I'd heard the words before, but until then they had never meant anything.

"Oh Yah" was proud of his car and what he had done to it though it was ten years old or more at the time. But this was in the late '20s and an auto, any auto, was a wondrous invention to those of his generation.

We chugged along at a speed of twenty miles per hour, bouncing along to the beat of the four-cycle motor. We passed Colbert's place and "Oh Yah" waved grandly to Colbert, the ice cream man, who happened to be out with his cattle. Colbert had but a small spread, but he made the finest ice cream to sell to the summer people on Saturdays and Sundays. Ice cream made from cream that was so thick you had to spoon it out of the bottle. He also sold milk and cream.

Then we came to Ted McCracken's Last Hope Ranch, a poor forty acre homestead that barely supported his wife and ragamuffin children who came shrieking out to the road to wave at us as we sailed by. Ted was a handyman for one of the resorts at Luby Bay.

We circumvented the last serpentine curve in the road, rolled out over a log trestle that traversed a marsh and on to the county road. The trestle was similar to a railroad trestle, only the tracks were of logs flattened on the upper surface with a raised log on the two inner sides to prevent an auto or logging truck from slipping off into the bottomless mud of the marsh.

The trestle was solidly built, but it didn't seem to be a sure thing that you wouldn't slip off. The Model T was light-weight. It bounced when it hit the slightest obstruction. And the front wheels wobbled. It was not a confidence builder, and I was relieved when we reached the county road. From there it was but a short distance to Luby Bay.

Long before he reached the bay he sounded his air horn and the eerie wail reverberated through the hills and down the road announcing his imminent arrival. "Pays to advertise," he said to me with his gold-toothed grin.

The bed of his truck was loaded with strawberries and vegetables he raised for sale to the summer people. The soil on his hillside was sandy, ideal for growing strawberries. Across the road from his barn the soil was rich and black, and there he had his vegetable garden. The growing season being short the only vegetables that did well were potatoes, radishes and lettuce. Around his garden he built a six foot high fence of poles and shakes to keep the deer out.

Upon arrival at our cottage, "Oh Yah" stepped down and the children ran to greet him. He removed the tray, filled with little cartons of strawberries and vegetables, from the truck bed, suspended it from one shoulder with a loop of rope and was off like the Pied Piper of Hamelin, the children bounding all about him. They'd gather just to hear him say, "Yah, yah, oh yah." He cherished their attention and affection.

Invariably "Oh Yah" picked his strawberries too soon, and they would be partly white and partly red. The housewives would complain and then say, "The poor man has to make a living," and put the berries in the sun to ripen. There was little fresh fruit in the Kaniksu at the time.

A school teacher visited "Oh Yah" in the summer, and the two would pick huckleberries. What they couldn't eat or preserve, they'd sell. Then one winter "Oh Yah" trapped beaver from his pond to be made into a fur coat for her. The game warden caught him in the act of trapping beaver without a license for which he served sixty days in the county jail in Priest River. He couldn't —

or perhaps wouldn't — pay the fine, being a frugal man.

It was rumored that "Oh Yah" strayed over onto Forest Service land when harvesting timber from his land. But the early ones in the Kaniksu — having been there long before game wardens and the United States Forest Service — were accustomed to taking the forest gifts for their own use. So it was easy to forgive "Oh Yah" for these minor trespasses.

When someone did a special favor for "Oh Yah," he'd offer to buy the person a drink. The two of them would repair to Millie's bar, the person beaming brightly and talking animatedly in anticipation of a few rounds of whiskey.

"Oh Yah" would march up to the bar and announce grandly, "The drinks are on me."

The bartender would ask respectfully, "What's your pleasure, Elmer?"

And he would reply, "A bottle of beer and two glasses, if you please."

The Kaniksu offered little promise of wealth to the early ones, but it cast a spell that held them a lifetime. It was a new country. It was unique. Three climatic regions come together; the subarctic, the Rocky Mountain, and the Pacific. This produced a rare combination of plants and animals and fish. There were yew, white pine, ponderosa pine, cedar, tamarack, hemlock, birch, alpine fir and white bark pine. There were grizzly bear and black bear and mule deer and white-tail deer and woodland caribou and mountain lions and mountain goats. In the streams and lakes were cutthroat trout, dolly varden and westslope whitefish. Strains of mushrooms found nowhere else developed over the eons of time. There were no poisonous plants nor snakes. In the forest was a unique orange caterpillar, black at both ends and orange in the middle. It was a veritable paradise.

"Oh Yah" lived out his life in the Kaniksu. He led a quiet, unremarkable life. He won no wars. He didn't rise to the presidency. But he was a happy man. He was found one day sitting on his chopping block, his back against his woodpile. He had died looking out over his beloved valley.

The author has included a collection of old photographs on the following pages that he hopes will help the reader place the events of the stories in proper times and location in the great Northwest. It will also serve to satisfy a sense of nostalgia for this romantic and adventurous period in the author's youth.

Jim Low and author in dugout canoe hewn out of a cedar log by Jim, circa 1924.

B.R.C. Camp 272 with pack string in front of cooking and mess tent.

Lolo Ranger Station circa 1936.

The crew at Lolo Ranger station. From left are Joe Schmidt, Carroll Lundegren, Dewey Duffel, Ross Middlemist, Darrell Weaver and Clarence Willey.

Ross Middlemist, packer on the Lolo Ranger District.

The author at Mormon Lookout.

Ross Middlemist with lead mule, Babe.

The author and Ross Middlemist revisit West Fork Butte Lookout.

Hunt Lake high in the Selkirk Mountains.

Left: Crest of the Selkirk Mountains. Below: The author fly fishing on Dinty's pond.

Part Two

STORIES
OF THE
BITTERROOTS

Chapter 8

AS EVER YOUR FRIEND, CHARLIE SCHWARTZ

CHARLIE'S LETTER AND THE WORDS HAVE BEEN FOLLOWING ME around for over fifty years, and they were good words and Charlie Schwartz was one hell of a man.

Charlie was kind enough to say in his letter that he did not for a minute blame me for taking a part in the "unfortunate occurrence" on Gold Creek and that he'd like to hear from me again.

I never wrote. I did try to call him in later years in Avon, Idaho, but the operator said there was no Charles Schwartz listed for Avon. I've wondered what happened to his assistant, "Tin Pants," and the camp orator and the tough little lumberjack who played such important parts in the "unfortunate occurrence."

I've wondered, too, if there would be any sign of B.R.C. Camp 272 left. Tucked up against the Bitterroot wall as it was, perhaps a pole or two from the tent frames or a board from Charlie's stoop escaped a hunter's or fisherman's fire.

With his black high-heeled White Loggers, black Levi's, and his black domed hat, he looked seven feet tall standing on that stoop, his assistant "Tin Pants" backing him up.

There were thirty of us facing him down and his only expression was a slight frown as our spokesman edged out from the crowd.

The summer had started out well enough. The trip over from Spokane was exciting: crossing northern Idaho on the Milwaukee Railroad, through the great tunnel under the Bitterroot Mountains and into Montana; looking back across the switchbacks at the orange caterpillar-like tail of the train as we graded down to the Clark Fork River; seeing the double row of brown, weathered buildings on the bench across the river; the conductor saying it was a ghost town, a watering spot for miners, cowboys, lumberjacks, now sitting quietly in its retirement; the conductor announcing St. Regis, Mont., and me looking out the window and seeing nothing but mountains and river; getting off the train and then seeing the steel bridge spanning the Clark Fork River and a dusty road leading up to a cluster of wooden buildings; no one there to meet me; welcome to St. Regis; it growing dark and me feeling lonely; "Tin Pants" finally showing up and us backtracking over the Bitterroot in a pickup truck to road's end at the St. Joe River; hiking nine miles up Gold Creek with pack on back to B.R.C. Camp 272, B.R.C. being the Blister Rust Corps of the U.S. Forest Service.

Back in that world of trees and mountains and clear streams, it was so peaceful and beautiful and quiet. When you'd come out and hear a truck clanking up the road, you'd think you couldn't stand the harsh sound and want to flee back up the trail. It took you days to get used to city noises again.

The work was easy enough. We grubbed out the ribes, which were wild current bushes, in an attempt to save the great white pine forest of Idaho. The parasite causing the blister rust of the white pine had a life cycle from the ribes to the white pine and back to the ribes. By removing the ribes we broke the cycle.

Charlie and "Tin Pants" — we called him that because he wore waterproofed khaki tin pants, permanently bent at the knee — would take us out to the work areas. They had previously run lines of white string up the mountain sides marking off each crew's work area.

Our crew was made up of myself; two other forestry students, Olie and Simmons from the University of Idaho; and Sam, a lumberjack. The days blended into a simple routine of breakfast, hit the trail, be at the work area by eight, grubbing out the ribes until noon, the half hour lunch, back to grubbing out ribes, return to camp by 4:30 and dinner at 5.

The work could be handled by two percent of the brain while the rest went into neutral and floated off into daydreams that would become stories you would tell yourself. You were so far from the sounds of cars and airplanes and trains and crowds, you drifted into a world of unreality. A world that offered a false sense of security. A gentle trap that dulled the ambition and then dumped the working stiff out once again on city streets with a bedroll over his shoulder and a few dollars in his pocket.

You lived in tents, ate huge meals, washed your clothes and cut wood for your sheepherder stoves. It was like one extended camping trip except that you got board and room and $80 a month. We would talk about the dudes over on the dude ranches out of Missoula paying $80 a week for the same privileges.

The meals were unbelievable. The work encouraged large scale appetites. The cook would announce breakfast by beating on an iron triangle that hung outside the cook tent, and you'd better hustle up there. The long picnic style table would be heaped with pancakes, slab bacon, ham, eggs, hash browns, biscuits, jams, cake, pie, canned fruit and coffee that could float a horseshoe.

Lunch you put together yourself from a table loaded with sandwich makings, cookies, small tins of fruit, all of which you put in a used sugar sack and tied to your belt.

Dinner. Again the table was heaped with pies, cookies, cakes, canned fruit, platters of canned meats, ham, fresh meats and vegetables — if the pack train came in that day, otherwise two or three canned vegetables — mashed potatoes, fresh baked bread and biscuits, tinned butter, and coffee.

There was little talk at the table, mostly pass this or that and little of that talk because the food was speared mostly by knife, making dinner a sporting event. One of the lumberjacks was so accomplished with the knife he ate peas with it.

Living in tents added to the illusion of being on a grand camping trip. The tents were white canvas, strung tight under a framework of lodgepole pine poles. There was a sheepherder sheet-metal stove to take the chill off mountain evenings. In each corner was a wood and canvas fold-up army cot with a sleeping bag rolled up at one end. You could lean against it and read the pulp magazines. Sleeping bags were to be rolled up unless you were sleeping in them. Charlie's rules.

The floor of the tent was earth carpeted with grass, with the exception of Charlie's. As camp boss, he rated a built up wooden floor and wooden stoop.

You lived out of your Trapper Nelson pack board. Things you used daily, like flashlight, metal mirror, towels, hat, you hung on willow rods held by ties to the tent wall. You washed and shaved in a metal basin with water from Gold Creek.

Saturday was wash day, shirts and socks only. Your Levi's became so stiff they could stand in a corner by themselves. Sundays were for fly fishing on Gold Creek which ran alongside camp or on the

St. Joe which involved an eighteen mile round trip hike. Or you could explore some of the trails and pick huckleberries and thimbleberries. You might turn a corner and run into a black bear or cow moose with calf. The former would high-tail it, but the latter might give you a few anxious moments.

The woods, which had been so moist in June, turned tinder dry in late July. The warm sunny days had been good, but they and the lack of rain dried out the forest. A dropped match or a spark from a sheepherder stove could explode into a roaring inferno before anyone could stop it.

One such fire occurred at a logging camp when a spark from a donkey engine flew into some slashings. Even with a half dozen men nearby to fight it, it took off and burned a hundred thousand acres before it could be brought under control.

So Charlie placed a ban on smoking in the woods and fires in our sheepherder stoves. The camp turned in on itself, and the mood became as explosive as the parched woods around us.

Then one night in early August diarrhea hit camp. A cramping and horrendous urge woke me. I had slept in my shorts, but there was not time to dress, and I fled down the trail to the camp latrine.

It was a silvery, bright-as-day moonlight night but no Bobby Burns "Where danced the moon on Monan's Rill." It was more of a Lord Tennyson "Into the valley of death rode the six hundred."

For all about me, I saw the moon flashing on bare asses hung over bushes, over logs, over stumps, and on desperate forms clutching any available tree trunk. There was no comparison to today's car filled with kids performing a one- two- or even the very rare three-bare-ass mooning. Ten, fifteen perhaps even as many as twenty asses beamed in the moonlight.

The four hole open latrine was fully manned. Someone threw a roll of john paper to me and I joined the troops.

It took several hours for the scourge to run its course, but finally toward dawn peace settled over camp. Not a man had been spared. Charlie went from tent to tent administering paregoric and determining the extent of the damage. He decided we were all too weak to work and declared the day a legal holiday.

The temper of the camp became even more volatile. There was grumbling, and threats were made to the cook and his helper. Whether or not this thing is caused by bad food or a virus, the cook and helper are always accused of not getting enough soap off the dishes, and we blamed them for the catastrophe.

The next weekend Charlie let two of the boys from the orator's tent wangle permission to drive to Missoula. They came back to camp a day late, and he fired them. The match had dropped.

The next morning, just before going out to work, one of the men came to our tent, lifted the flap and said, "We're holding a meeting and want you to join us."

We didn't think much of it, though this was unusual. Curiosity getting the better of us, we went over to the orator's tent to see what was going on.

The orator was a fat little guy. Kind of greasy and I had never liked him. He ran a pan card game in his tent on weekends and won so often that some of the boys had accused him of cheating. He started talking in a disarming way. "These are the two boys here that Charlie fired. Believe me, they couldn't help getting back to camp late. They had car trouble.

"Now we think we all ought to go up to Charlie and tell him we think he's being too hard on these boys. They need the job, and we'll ask him to take them back. What do you say?"

It seemed reasonable, so we all gathered around Charlie's tent, and a tough little lumberjack was sent up to the flap and invited Charlie out.

Charlie stood with his feet widespread, that black domed hat riding high on his head and the rim smooth and flat.

There were thirty of us facing Charlie down, and the orator edged out from the crowd.

"Charlie," he said, "we don't think it's fair of you to fire these two boys. Either you take them back or we're walking out."

My God, he'd gone too far.

Charlie looked around at the crowd and said, "Do you all feel the same way?"

It seemed a bit late to be backing out. No one wanted to appear yellow, and no one spoke out.

Charlie stood quietly, eyeing us individually, his voice turned cold and he said, "OK boys. Pack your gear. Hit the trail." He turned and went back into his tent.

We were putting our gear together when Charlie stepped into our tent and asked if we were sure that this was the way we wanted it. I didn't want it, but the psychology of the moment was such that I couldn't back out. Simmons and Olie and I had been too shocked to talk it over, but I think they felt the same as I. Someone mumbled, "I guess we're still agreed."

Charlie shook our hands and said, "No hard feelings," and left. Sam said nothing. If he had, we could have stayed without losing face.

Sam waited until we had stopped halfway down the trail at a spring for a drink and a "five." He smoked a roll-your-own Bull Durham, and as we shouldered our packs, quietly said, "You know, those two really didn't have car trouble. They hung one on in Missoula and came back to camp drunk." Why had he waited 'til there was no turning back to tell us?

I wrote to Charlie later in the summer telling him of my feelings

and regrets about the "unfortunate occurrence" and this is the letter
he wrote to me:

B.R.C. Camp 272

Dear Tom,

*I received your letter, and want you to know that I cer-
tainly appreciate your writing to me. It was a mighty fine
thing for you to do.*

*I did not for a minute blame you for taking an active
part in the unfortunate occurrence.*

*Your only mistake, Tom, was in allowing another to
speak for you. I believe if you had stopped and thought the situation over thoroughly, you would have seen this at the time.
In the future (pardon the lecture) think for yourself, and back
your judgement against any crowd. For it is a proven fact that
a crowd cannot reason.*

*Perhaps the best thing we can do is forget all of the affair,
except what can be useful to us in a like emergency. I know
that I got a few lessons myself.*

*I would like to hear from you again, and if you are back
at Moscow next term, may see you as I go there quite frequent-
ly.*

As ever your friend,

Charlie Schwartz

Charlie never came to Moscow, and I became busy with my
studies and did not write again.

I have kept his letter for over fifty years. It is one of those things you can never bring yourself to discard and small enough baggage to carry with you, to take out and touch, and know that the time and the place were real and they were good.

The Blister Rust Corps was to last but a few years more and then it became just a period of time and a memory.

Chapter 9

THE WIDOWMAKER

"THAT WAS A WIDOW MAKER, TOMMY," ROSS SAID. WE HAD JUST started the backcut on the lightning struck weathered old snag when a great gray limb tore loose and ghosted to the ground between us. We hadn't heard it coming. A foot to the left and it would have crushed our skulls.

Ross Middlemist was the packer at the Lolo Ranger Station, headquarters for the Lolo Ranger District in the Bitterroot Mountains south and west of Missoula, Mont. The year was 1939.

Earlier in the day, Ross and Dewey Duffel, a lookout like myself, and I had been on trail crew up the South Fork of Lolo Creek. We had cleared a couple of miles of trail and rehung telephone lines and had stopped for a "five." We found a smooth old log to sit on, and Dewey lit up a roll-your-own Bull Durham cigarette.

If you've never seen one, it's a thin limp thing you build yourself from a packet of light tan cigarette papers and a bag of Bull Durham tobacco. You pour tobacco onto the paper, roll it up, twist the two ends and hang it from the corner of your mouth. Once lit you can't take it from your mouth or the tobacco falls out and you've got a fire.

So Dewey sat there squinting, the smoke curling up, his eye smarting. I asked, "How can you stand those things?"

And he replied, "They're tobacco and they're cheap and they taste good." I tried one once, and it was the foulest thing I ever put into my mouth.

Ross was putting a razor edge on his double bitted ax, and when he finished held the whetstone out to me and said, "You better sharpen that brush hook. Looks a little dull."

Ross was the leader of the group. He was a woodsman, who had worked for the Forest Service in the summers, and as a jack in the logging camps in the winters. Though he was but five feet five inches, he could stand up to big Clarence Willey our alternate ranger who wrestled professionally in the off season.

I was putting the finishing touches to the edge of the brush hook, a wicked looking tool the size of an ax with a heavy flat hook at the end, when I noticed Dewey straighten up and look down trail.

"Someone's coming," Dewey said. Probably a fisherman, I thought. And then Carroll Lundegren, who was the station dispatcher, came into view. I felt a little uneasy sitting down on the job. But Carroll said, "Don't get up boys. I'll have a cigarette and fiver with you."

"What are you doing up this way?" Ross asked.

"A big storm is coming in from the west," Carroll replied, "dropping lightning over in the Lochsa-Selway wilderness area.

"Lots of fires in the Powell Ranger District," he said and then, "Probably hit us late tonight. We'll need every man we've got to fight fires. So we're going to have to break camp and get back to the ranger station."

We picked up our gear and hurried back to camp and soon had the tent down. Ross wrapped the food and gear in manties and lashed them down on his mules. Ross could take a pack that Dewey and I together would have a hard time lifting, swing it up off the ground, slap it on a mule and lash it down.

It was a nine mile hike to the Lolo Road where Carroll had left the stake truck to take Dewey and me back to the ranger station. Ross would follow on horse with his string of mules.

Shortly after dinner, Darrell Weaver, the district ranger, came over to the station house. Darrell had grown up on a ranch and preferred to wear a cattleman's khaki pants and shirt and Stetson to the official U.S.F.S. olive green uniform. I often wondered how this went over with the regional office in Missoula.

It was getting dark by then and Darrell said, "You better hit the hay and get as much sleep as you can. It's going to be a long night."

Dewey and Ross and I went up to the bunk room which took up the entire second floor. It looked much like an army barracks. The floor was bare pine and there were a number of iron cots with flat springs and thin mattresses on top. We threw our sleeping bags down on them.

I had scarcely gotten to sleep when I was shaken awake. Ross whispered, "Darrell is sending you and me over to a fire on Fish Creek. A report has just come through from Wendover's of a big burning snag just off the Fish Creek Road."

Wendover was a rancher who had a cattle spread at road's end along Fish Creek. He would be called on to fight fire later in the night. The cattle business was still slow following the Depression and ranchers in the district supplemented their income fighting fire.

Ross and I had slept fully dressed, so all we had to do was to pull on our boots, put two fire packs and a crosscut saw in the bed of a pickup truck and take off up the Lolo Creek Road.

There were a couple of lights on at Lolo Hot Springs, a rustic resort built around a series of hot mineral pools, when we passed by. Lewis and Clark camped here on their return trip from the Pacific on June 29, 1806. Other than these lights the night was black, the velvet blackness after a lightning storm has passed.

Shortly after passing the hot springs, we turned off on the Fish Creek Road. It was narrow, winding and slippery from the rain that accompanied the storm. The truck's headlights were dim and revealed but a short stretch of the road. Ross hunched over the steering wheel, peering ahead for obstructions in the road — fallen limbs or a fallen tree. We didn't talk, each totally absorbed in the unwinding road.

The road rose up a series of switchbacks to a divide and then angled sharply down into the Fish Creek country. Here the forest was second growth dotted with tall gray snags from an old fire. We drove for some time and were beginning to wonder if we had missed the fire. Finally from an overview we could see the burning snag on a bench across Fish Creek. It looked like fireworks, burning brightly and throwing sparks into the black night.

Here the road had become a single track hung on the east wall of Fish Creek. We found a pullout and Ross parked the pickup. We shouldered our firepacks and felt our way down to the creek bottom. Ross trailered the two-man crosscut saw behind. The creek was not wide but was swollen from melting snow at the source. The bed was cobbled with large boulders, and the footing was treacherous. In the blackness we had no idea how deep the water was, but there was only one way to go — across — and we plunged in. We staggered about like two drunks, but by leaning upstream in the deep parts and flailing our arms about when we stumbled we were able to reach the far bank.

We searched about and found a ravine that led upwards in the general direction of the fire. We came out within a hundred yards of the snag. It lit up a hole in the blackness. Fire was creeping down the trunk, and a wind was scattering sparks over the hillside and starting spot fires.

We placed our fire packs in a spot away from the falling sparks and hurriedly untied the tarps from the wooden pack frames and spread out the fire tools: shovels; mattocks, a tool with an ax at one end of the head and a chisel-like wedge at the other for loosening the earth; and two two-gallon canvas water bags. Simple but nourishing food rations were also included.

What had looked like a bench from the road, turned out to be an open rocky hillside with sparse bunches of grass and wispy shrubs. Beyond was second growth forest that reached far above to the skyline. And here and there we could see other more exposed snags sticking out above the forest. It was a mystery why the lightning had struck this particular one.

It was in the clumps of grass that the falling sparks had started spot fires. These we had to hit first before they could run together and take off up the mountainside. We each took a shovel and threw cool earth on them. Then we turned our attention to the snag.

We made an undercut with the crosscut saw on the uphill side of the snag and notched it out with one of the mattocks. From time to time we would have to stop and put out new fires in the grasses from the still flying sparks.

Ross placed the mattock in the notch with the handle pointing uphill which indicated the direction the snag would fall. At first he was not satisfied, notched one side deeper, and this time the handle pointed where he wanted to fell the tree. We then made a down-slanting cut on the downhill side of the tree which would force it to fall uphill and anchor it down.

The sawing was slow and tedious because the snag was hard and resinous and the saw would bind. We had hardly started the back-cut when the first dead limb ghosted down between us.

"What do we do now?" I asked.

"We keep sawing, but we keep an eye on the limbs above us," he replied.

That was not wholly reassuring, because by the time we would see a limb coming it would be too late to get out of the way. Maybe, I thought, we might be able to slip our heads out of the way. I didn't want Ross to think I was uneasy about the whole operation and grabbed the handle and started sawing. Ross had the lightest, smoothest touch on a two man saw. With him, the saw just floated back and forth, and you didn't get worn down.

Other limbs ghosted down, but not near us. Ross finally shout-ed "timber," and we leaped away from the snag, Ross with the saw. The snag fell uphill as planned, but when it hit the ground it vibrated a few times and then shot downhill. I thought Oh my God, we'll have fire all the way to Fish Creek.

It came to rest a hundred yards below us, showering fire as it went. Again we snuffed these fires out with cool earth.

Then we tackled the fire in the snag. We threw dirt on the flames with the shovels, and they would go out. We'd move on. But fire would pop up again, the resin reacting like the chemicals in trick matches. We just couldn't get ahead of it.

It was getting light and Ross said, "Tommy, why don't you take the water bags, fill them at the nearest water and we'll try to drown the fire."

I was glad to get away from the fire and smoke and rinse the ashes and dirt off my face and arms, get a drink and cool off. There was a rivulet in the ravine and I found a pool not far below. First I drank the water. More than I should have, because it was icy and I was overheated and it made me queasy. I filled the two bags and walked slowly up the hill. We'd had little or no sleep in twenty-four hours, had cleared trail and hiked nine miles the previous day and fought fire for over six hours.

Ross took a deep drink from one of the bags when I returned and then poured the rest on a small portion of the fire. It sizzled and steam rose, but this time the fire stayed out. We took turns going after water.

At last the fire in the great snag was out. A little steam still rose, but the flames and smoke were gone and we had the fire under control. We retrieved our rations, sat on our tarps, ate, rested and watched the blackened snag. Our ration packs contained a tin of beef, hardtack, raisins, and tins of peaches. We ate the beef on pieces of hardtack and washed it down with the cold spring water. The peaches were cool and sweet and felt smooth sliding down our throats. The packet of raisins we savored, one at a time.

We stayed with the fire another hour, felt the snag all over for hot spots, but it was cold, the fire out. Then we searched the area for spark-started fire, but all the blackened spots were cool. The snag would no longer steam when we poured water in the cracks.

We put our firepacks back together. They would be gone-over at the station — the rations replaced, the shovels, the mattocks and the saw cleaned and sharpened for the next fire.

We stopped at Fish Creek on our return to the pickup and washed off our blackened faces and arms and drank from the icy waters. This time the water soothed and cooled our legs as we forded the stream. I sloshed carelessly across. At this point I would have welcomed a dunking.

It was easier climbing out than it had been coming down in the dark. It seemed less formidable, and we could use the scrubby bushes growing there to pull ourselves up in the steeper parts. We were moving slower. You need to pace yourself when fighting fire or it consumes you and drains your strength away. But this one, with the fire creeping down the trunk of the snag and the wind scattering sparks over the hillside and starting other fires, had goaded us into working at too fast a pace.

By the time we reached the road and the pickup, it was well past noon. We dumped the firepacks into the truck's bed and took a last look across Fish Creek. There was no smoke rising in the now still air. It was peaceful. The storm had passed. There was a blue sky overhead and white puffs of cloud moving lazily across.

Chapter **10**

TRAIL CREW

TRAIL CREW, THE RITE OF SPRING THAT CAME AFTER THE SNOW had gone from all but the darkest ravines and highest peaks, was a time to rehang the No. 9 telephone wire and clear the trails in the backcountry of the Lolo Ranger District — trails that seemed as permanent as the rocky outcropping that flanked them.

I thought the trails would be there forever and would have been astounded to know how many would become U.S.F.S. fire roads and access routes for loggers who would defoliate large areas of the Lolo Ranger District. But I had not yet noticed nor understood the logic of change. Nor did I realize how unique the moment was; that it would not be repeated and that it was a turning point in larger affairs. World War II was just around the corner and nothing would be the same again.

The trails wound through the forest like rivers, each bend with its own mystery and revelation; a hillside bright with Indian paintbrush, a beaver meadow dusted with white daisies, a tree-framed peak in the distance, a black bear pulling apart a rotted log, or a belligerent cow elk with calf that considered the trail her own.

There were four of us in the crew that summer. There was Ross Middlemist, Dewey Duffel, who was a lookout like myself, and a CCC worker whose name I cannot recall but will refer to as "Droopy."

We lived in a tent that Ross moved up trail every day or two so that the time required to walk to work was kept to a minimum. We slept on the ground in government issue Kapok sleeping bags that scarcely disguised the hard ground. We cooked our meals over an open fire.

Ross did much of the cooking. Mornings he was the first up and would have a fire started and a pot of strong, black coffee bubbling. Meals were limited to what could be cooked in a frying pan or hung over the fire in a pot; lots of ham and eggs, beans, soups, and stews. It didn't matter, because you worked hard and were hungry, and it filled the corners of your stomach.

Droopy was always the last one out of the tent in the morning. He wore army olive drab shirts and pants and army shoes. The rest of us wore blue work shirts, Levi's, White boots and felt hats. Ross wore the black Stetson, the mark of a packer. Droopy worked as little as possible, but perhaps was worth the paltry wages paid him. He came from the Bronx. He constantly complained about the quiet and the lack of girls. He missed the crowded streets, the cab drivers and the buses. He didn't last long on the district.

Dewey was a wiry little man who was always hitching up pants that rode low on his thin hips. He put in a full day's work. He had been on his own from the time he was twelve years old. That was the last time he attended school. He picked oranges and grapefruit in the winter in Phoenix. He drove an ancient black touring car, and I often wondered how he ever got from Phoenix, Ariz., to Lolo, Mont., and back. He considered himself an expert pan player. In the fall when he received his summer wages, he hit the gambling parlors in Missoula. He invariably lost his money and Ross would stake him the gas to drive to Phoenix.

Clearing the trails was simple work. We sawed passageways through trees that had fallen across them over winter. We trimmed limbs and encroaching brush to a width and height that would not touch a skittery mule nor knock the hat off a rider on horseback.

On a typical day we'd be up by six and hit the trail by 7:30. Ross would carry the two man crosscut saw, Dewey a double-bitted ax, I the brush hook and Droopy the tree climbing outfit. We worked at a methodical pace, taking an occasional fiver to avoid becoming overly tired and careless. The tools were honed to wickedly sharp edges. A moment's carelessness could result in an injury, and we were far from medical attention. Despite these precautions, accidents did happen.

The second day out Dewey burned a tree. We had come upon a great ponderosa pine. At its base the telephone line lay loosely, brought down by a snag blown across it over winter. Ross and I sawed a section from the snag, and Droopy helped roll it out of the way freeing the line.

Meanwhile Dewey had put on the tree climbing spurs and climbing belt. The belt lacked three feet of going around the tree trunk, so Ross spliced on a piece of telephone wire. Ross took the extended belt around the tree and attached it to the other side of Dewey's climbing outfit. I lifted the wire over Dewey's head and lay it across the belt. It was like suiting up a high-wire walker.

Dewey, looking a bit apprehensive, asked, "You sure this thing is going to hold together, Ross?"

"Absolutely," Ross replied.

Dewey started climbing, first punching the left spurred boot into the thick-barked tree, then the right, lifting the belt and wire as he went. The bark was so thick it was hard for him to get a good bite of wood. The whole operation was beginning to look like climbing a stairway to the stars with Dewey looking more worried the higher he got.

He stopped at twenty feet, perched like a pileated woodpecker on the side of the tree. He had no trouble attaching an insulator and the line to the tree, but when he leaned back to get a better angle to hack off a limb that touched the telephone line, his spurs pulled loose from the extra pressure put on them.

Dewey shot down the tree held tightly to it by the climbing belt, the rough bark burning his chest, his spindly arms flailing about as he tried to clutch the tree and arrest his fall. It was like a Laurel and Hardy routine. Even though the performer was taking a beating, it was one of the most comical sights you'd ever see. But you couldn't laugh. We presented a funeral director's pious concern. We asked the miserable, tangled heap, "You OK? Can we go to camp and get the first aid kit?"

And he replied in righteous indignation, "Hell no! Just get me a little spring water so I can wash the bark and blood out of these chest wounds you sanctimonious, hypocritical bastards."

So we stopped at the next icy rivulet that crossed the trail and Dewey bathed his wounds. Being mid-morning, we extended the stop into a long fiver.

We were high on the east slope of West Fork Butte and had a clear view down the South Fork of Lolo Creek. Beyond lay Blue Mountain and in plain view on one of its side ridges was the remains of the Old Woodman Lookout. It had been abandoned in the early '30s when lookouts were being built on the higher peaks that gave better views of the surrounding country.

The Woodman Lookout had been a log cabin. The valuable elements — roof boards, windows, iron stove, copper wire and lighting rod — had been removed and packed out by Ross and his string of mules. What remained resembled a hay manger.

Droopy asked, "What is that thing?"

Ross, a master of the put-on and the tall tale, said, "You heard of the great hay drop to feed the starving elk and deer?"

Droopy said yes, he had.

And then Ross explained in a confidential manner, "The animals would get up on top of the bales. They'd tromp all over them, and there would be a lot of waste. So the research boys hit on a plan to overcome the wastage. They decided to build mangers on the key winter ranges and because of their inaccessibility drop the hay into them by plane. They chose the old Ford Tri Motor plane for the job. They could fly low and slow over the mangers, and they had a high load capacity. Official estimates of the operation was 17,650 elk saved."

"What a humanitarian thing to do," Dewey put in.

"Yes, the service does have a heart," Ross said.

Droopy looked a little puzzled but seemed satisfied with the explanation and went back to work. About a half hour later he stopped in the middle of chopping on a log and said "God damn it! You're putting me on Middlemist. They couldn't have hit that manger with a bale of hay in a million years."

"They used the Nordum Bombsight," Ross said seriously, and once again Droopy was satisfied.

Days were good — one quiet, peaceful, unhurried day after another — the sunny ones just better. Showers we would wait out, but an all day rain would tie us up in camp. Logs and trails would then be slippery, and you need to slip only once when swinging a sharp ax or brush hook. Then we'd mend clothing, read, play cards and kill time.

One day we stopped for lunch on a high bench overlooking a narrow valley. We had finished eating and settled back against a large mossy log, not talking, just looking, enjoying the view when we heard a high pitched flute-like sound float across the valley. It had a sense of urgency to it.

"What in God's green earth is it?" I asked Ross.

"Sounds like an elk to me," Ross replied.

"Think you're right," Dewey agreed.

The sound seemed to be coming from a low ridge across the valley. We scanned the area for some time before catching a movement at the base of a large ponderosa pine. The tree had a high, bare trunk with branches densely bunched above. A cow elk was circling the tree. Shortly she left the tree and disappeared into a nearby brush-filled ravine.

A black bear scrambled down the tree trunk and made for the ravine. Immediately the elk charged out and drove the bear back up the tree. This was repeated several times, but at last the bear reached the cover of the ravine. The elk circled the ravine, bleating from time to time.

We watched until our lunch break was over and then had to get back to work clearing trail. We planned to check out the ravine on our way back to camp, but a heavy rain set in late in the afternoon. By the time we reached the spot again, the elk was no longer in view. We were drenched and cold, anxious to get back to camp and a dry change of clothing, so we did not stop. Often afterward, we would talk about the mysterious events and wonder if the cow had a calf hidden in the ravine. We would speculate that the bear had killed the calf, and the grieving cow, then duty relieved, left.

Another day Ross and I cleared a side trail to Skookum Butte Lookout, the southernmost in the district. The lookout was set at the edge of the butte, and from it you had a long view down the crest of the Bitterroots. Across the endless forest the snow capped Lolo and St. Joseph Peaks stood out on the horizon. Below us was the great Elk Meadows. It is such a remote area I expected to see elk grazing. But all through lunch we watched and no animals appeared. "They probably left the meadows early after first light and are holed up somewhere in the woods," Ross said.

Darrell Weaver, our district forest ranger, had ordered us to report in from Skookum Butte and give him a progress report. When Ross unlocked the single door to the lookout, we were met by a strong, musky animal odor.

Inside it was dark, the windows still covered by shutters that protected them from the gales of winter. We could just make out the old fashioned crank telephone hung on the fire finder pedestal. Ross hooked up the phone to the batteries and rang two longs and a short, the ranger station number. But the line was dead and we figured the batteries were gone. We closed and locked the door.

I started down the trail. Ross called out, "Hold it Tommy. We'll go back another way."

"What is it," I asked, wondering what Ross was up to. He'd once sent me off down the wrong side of a mountain.

"Something worthwhile. You'll see."

Then he plunged cross country down the butte, and I followed suspiciously but filled with curiosity. Shortly we came upon a narrow bench. Through the trees I could see a shallow pond in the middle of it.

Ross walked along the edge of the pond. He seemed to be searching for something, acting mysteriously, not answering when I asked what was going on. Finally he stopped and picked up a long, smooth, weathered lodgepole pine pole. He stepped boldly out into the pond and called for me to come out.

I followed cautiously through the knee deep tepid water, and when I caught up to him I could see he was standing beside an inverted cone-shaped, lavender hole in the floor of the pond. It was beautiful, yet as I looked into it, I had the eerie feeling that like a venus fly trap, it was something that could swallow me up if I stumbled into it. And I backed off.

I said to Ross in an awed whisper, "My God, what are they?"

And he answered, "Probably only the devil knows. Look like they reach to hell don't they?"

Then he raised the pole and plunged it down into the hole with all his strength. It went down, down under the surface without striking bottom and then shot back out. He repeated the maneuver at different holes but could never reach bottom. I was relieved when Ross finally strode across the pond to firm ground.

We paused a moment for a final look. "Let's keep this to ourselves, Ross," I said.

"Yes. They'd bulldoze a road in here. Build board walks out over the water. Put in gravel paths, popcorn stands. Sell hot dogs and cokes."

"A wilderness improvement job."

Our last camp was at Granite Lake. Like so many mountain lakes it could have been called Hidden Lake. If the trail hadn't led directly to it you might never find it. It was tucked away at the foot of Skookum Butte, nothing in the terrain to give it away. You walked up a slight rise and there it was, a beautiful blue-green gem set in towering dark green pines and fir.

At the far end of the lake, it was shallow and tules grew. Nearby was a pebbled beach that shelved out into the lake. There were evidences of other trail crews having camped there over the years; a levelled spot to pitch a tent, a circle of rocks for a cooking fire and a bale of hay. The bale of hay we quickly tore apart and spread on the ground as a mattress. Someone had nailed a crate to a tree for food storage. Otherwise it was untouched, twelve miles from the nearest road.

I wondered if the trail and campsite hadn't always been there and used by the Indians. I searched for artifacts along the beach but didn't find any.

Evenings after a hot day on the trail, we'd skinnydip in the icy waters. We'd come out looking like periwinkles, our necks and faces and forearms burned brown from the sun, the rest of our bodies turned blue white from the frigid water. There's nothing more comical looking than naked white men hobbling about a rocky beach on tender feet.

Several trails fanned out from Granite Lake. On what was to be my last day, we worked a trail up towards Lost Park. My turn came to rehang line that had hung from a tree that reached out over a ravine. It was the only tree on an otherwise bare slope. The only way to replace the line was to mount the tree upside down on the lower side.

I was petrified, never having been one to like heights. But under the goading eyes of Ross and Dewey, I had no choice. I moved out slowly hanging from the safety belt, my climbing spurs thrust deeply as possible into the skinny tree. I managed to rehang the wire and make it back to solid ground.

Then Ross roared with laughter, "Tommy, that was the shakiest piece of tree climbing I've ever had the pleasure of watching." I swear he set the whole thing up.

This was our thirteenth day out, and when we returned to camp, Carroll Lundegren was there. He asked why we hadn't called in, and we explained that we had tried at Skookum Butte but that the batteries to the phone were dead. Then he said that the ranger wanted me back at the station and that he was to replace me.

"He's sending you up on West Fork Butte. There will be a truck to pick you up at Lolo Creek in three hours, so you better hustle."

"Hot damn," I thought to myself. "I'll be on the best lookout in the district." West Fork Butte was a weather station as well as a lookout. A two-track had been bulldozed into it, so I could drive my Model B Ford Coupe up to it. In previous years I had been on Mormon Peak, reached only by foot or horseback. The original engine in the Model B had been replaced with a V-8. It was a muscular little car. It had a high clearance and could take me anywhere.

I shouldered my Packer Nelson packboard and hit the trail. It was almost 5 o'clock, and Clarence, the alternate ranger, would be at the trailhead at eight to pick me up. Clarence weighed about 220 pounds, not the kind of man you'd want to keep waiting.

The trail was downhill, and I ran part of the way. Except for one small incident, the hike was routine. I had been pushing rapidly down trail when I came to a hairpin bend in a dense stand of lodgepole pine. As I came around the bend, I almost ran into a cow moose with calf in the trail. The moose stared at me belligerently, and I didn't know whether to jump into a creek that bordered the trail or try to climb one of the skinny trees. Neither one offered much protection. After a moment or two she turned and ambled sedately off across the creek, the calf scrambling to keep up.

When I arrived at Lolo Road, I leaned my packboard against a tree and sat on a log to await Clarence. I heard a car coming in the distance and then a black dot with a streamer of dust trailing out behind it. It didn't slow down so I moved back in the woods to avoid the dust. The trees along the road were a light khaki color from the passing cars. Promptly at eight, Clarence pulled up in the station pickup. I threw the packboard in the truck bed and moved in with him.

Chapter 11

WEST FORK BUTTE

WEST FORK BUTTE WAS A HIGH, FLAT-TOPPED MOUNTAIN SET IN the middle of the Lolo Ranger District. On a rock outcrop at its north rim, sat West Fork Butte Lookout, a tiny white speck in a great emptiness.

I had driven up to the lookout from the Lolo Ranger Station in my little black Ford Coupe, up a series of switchbacks into the lonely highcountry.

My first impression of the lookout was that it resembled a child's white, square building block with a black pyramid block set on top. And on the pyramid were stenciled the numerals 255. The trail to the lookout was cobbled with rock slabs, and as I walked up to it, I felt the loneness, the foreverness of the mountains.

It was quiet and the only voice I heard was at the end of a No. 9 telephone line when I reported my arrival to the ranger station nine miles below me in the Lolo Valley. I was used to hearing human voices, and I kept my battery powered radio turned on. The voice of the announcer, the sound of music, took the edge off my loneliness.

My radio reached the station in Missoula during the day and stations in Spokane and as far away as Denver at night. The Missoula station aired early Western music — cow camp songs like "Santa Fe Trail", "Strawberry Roan", and "Blood on the Saddle." I formed a lifelong liking for them.

The loneliness wore off after a day or two. Clarence had sent his black cocker spaniel up with me because she was in heat, and Darrell's mongrel dog was in love with her. Black Dog and I would sit on a rock slab at our doorstep after dinner and watch the sunset colors run up and down the Bitterroots, changing St. Joseph's and St. Mary's peaks from white to orange and disappear in the west over Lolo Pass. Then Black Dog and I would move inside, and I would light the Coleman gas lamp and read from the lookout's library of Western pulp magazines.

Some evenings I'd stand out there and sing as loudly as I could, my voice carrying out over the mountain. A psychiatrist might question my behavior, but I suspect it was no more irrational nor illogical than singing in the shower. Other evenings Black Dog and I would sit and watch the nighthawks on a feeding binge swooping up and about. When they would dive they'd make a noise like when you blow across a bottle opening. We'd watch the rock conies scurrying over the rocks, chirping in their high squeaky voices.

From West Fork Butte, I was looking down on history. For below me was the Lolo Trail, the ancient route of the Nez Perce Indians to the buffalo hunting grounds to the east. Lewis and Clark accompanied by the Shoshoni Indian woman, Sacajawea, followed this trail up Lolo Creek over Lolo pass on their way to the Pacific in 1805 and on their return trip in 1806.

Early each morning the sun splashed the peaks with orange, poured through my windows and gently waked me. First I scanned the mountains for sign of fire. Then I would report into the ranger station. After that I could dress, wash and cook breakfast. Breakfast was the big meal of the day; french toast or pancakes with ham or thick slices of ranch bacon and donuts. Donuts I cooked each Saturday morning, enough to last all week. You soon learn to cook on a lookout, or you starve. Black Dog ate the scraps.

A grizzly bear shared West Fork Butte with us. He would tear my garbage pit apart and feed on the scraps that Black Dog turned down. After rebuilding the wooden covering to the pit, I came up with a plan to keep him out. I would put large boulders on top of it. With a pry bar I moved several large slabs onto the wood covering.

The next morning Black Dog and I went down to inspect the pit. Garbage was strewn about, and the pit was wide open. The bear must have been extremely strong, for I found one large slab fifty feet or more downhill in the timber. He must have sent it there with one powerful swipe of a paw. I could see the bear had the upper hand. So I told Black Dog that we'd share the pit with the grizzly the remainder of our stay at West Fork Butte and left everything as we had found it.

The lookout was sparsely furnished; two straight back chairs, two metal beds that were to be folded up against the wall during the day, a small table, the cast-iron stove, and in the center of the room the firefinder mounted on a cast-iron pedestal.

The firefinder is the business end of the lookout. It comprises a round table with a map oriented to north on its surface, a brass rim etched with the 360 degrees of a circle on it, and a sighting mechanism called an "alidade" that revolves around the surface. Between the two uprights of the alidade is stretched a wire. You line the alidade up on the smoke. The wire intercepts the calibrated brass rim giving you the degrees or azimuth of the fire. You phone this reading into the ranger station. They plot your reading along with readings from other lookouts on their map, and where the lines cross is the precise location of the fire.

The USFS provided Bon Ami soap for washing windows. Bon Ami is the devil's playmate. It not only turns white when it dries, it sticks to the glass. So you go over each pane microscopically with a dry cloth, again and again. The leftover water you use to wash the floors, furniture, tools, your boots, your socks and your blue jeans. Water is a priceless commodity on a lookout. I got my water from a spring a mile down the mountainside. That's a long way when you're packing it uphill in a two-gallon canvas water bag in each hand and a six-gallon pack on your back. Water weighs eight pounds per gallon. So early on you become a water miser. When you return to civilization, you can't stand the sound of water running wastefully in a sink.

I would go for water every other day in the evenings when the forest had cooled down and the fire danger was low. I had to call the station for permission to leave the lookout. This was for my protection. If I didn't report in on my return, someone would come up to check on me.

One evening Black Dog and I were sauntering down the spring trail and ran into a black bear ambling up the trail. His nose was held just a few inches off the trail, and his head swayed from side to side. Normally I would not have been concerned over a black bear, but somewhere I had heard that dogs are one of their favorite meals. He kept coming closer and closer, and I was about to pick up Black Dog and climb the nearest tree when he stopped. For a few anxious moments, he looked us over. Then with a snort, he plunged off the trail and crashed down the mountainside.

Early in the mornings when the fire danger was down, I would work outside. There was always some work to be done. There was wood to chop and kindling to split, the building to be painted, and always the windows to be washed. Being caught with paint-filled, dry paintbrushes was a firing offense. So I always cleaned them with gasoline that was provided for the Coleman gas lamp. Then I washed them with Bon Ami, and they'd stay dry and soft.

The weather readings were to be taken in the early morning and evening. There was a rain gauge that measured the rainfall, a wind gauge, and a hygrometer that you whirled overhead to measure the humidity. Short round dowels were kept in a trench down by the turnaround where I kept my car. When weighed on a balance scale, the dowels gave an indication of the amount of moisture in the duff on the forest floor. These readings were used to measure the fire danger in the district.

Afternoons when the forest heated up and dried out, I had to be in my lookout watching for fires. I'd read, munch on oatmeal or sugar cookies that I baked on Saturdays, drink lemonade I made with cool water and citric acid and sugar. I kept my water cold by evaporation. There were shutters that extended out horizontally over the windows on all four sides of the lookout. I hung my water bags from the shutters and the ever present winds kept the water cold.

I'd think of Darrell down below at the ranger station: shuffling papers around, hoping he could make the figures come out right; hoping he could keep from burning down half his district; hoping he could keep his ass out of a jam with the forest supervisor. And here I was up here sipping lemonade, reading a magazine or a good book and enjoying the view.

The Forest Service was a world of men, a world run much like an army. The ranger was the commanding officer, the alternate ranger the executive officer, the dispatcher the adjutant, the packer the transportation officer, the lookouts the outposts, the smoke jumpers the parachute troops, and the fire fighters the reserves enlisted from the ranchers and migrant workers off the streets of Missoula.

The whole operation would move into action when the report would come down that a storm was moving into the Lolo. One mid-summer afternoon, Carroll Lundegren, the dispatcher, called to warn me that a heavy storm was moving in from the southwest and was expected to hit the district that evening. By early evening, I could see thunderheads building up beyond Lolo Pass. As they moved over the pass, lightning dropped out and danced along the crest of the Bitterroots lighting up the sky.

I watched, fascinated, as the strikes moved closer and closer. They reached the mountain across from me, marched down its near side and inexorably up the slope of West Fork Butte. The crashing and pounding built to a continuous roar. I felt a tingle of fear, for I had heard of lookouts who had been knocked unconscious when the lightning hit their lookouts.

I had been warned that the safest place during a lightning storm was the furthest point from any metal. That was along the wall near the door. So Black Dog and I moved over there and sat on the floor. I could just look over the windowsill and see where the lightning was hitting. The storm moved over us and suddenly, the air turned blue and I caught the smell of ozone. It is a penetrating smell, somewhat like a freshly struck match. A bolt of lightning had struck the lookout. But it had been safely dissipated by the lightning rod and heavy copper wires that ran down the corners of the roof and grounded out down the mountainside.

When the storm had moved safely beyond, I took readings with the alidade on two strikes that had flared up. One was a short way below me and the other on Graves Creek down in the valley. I reported the locations to Carroll. And he said, "They'll probably be put out by the rain, but keep an eye on them. We have had another report on the fire below you. Look for smoke when it gets light."

I was up at first light and saw a narrow column of smoke from the fire below me. It looked like an innocent campfire, but by late afternoon it could take out the lookout. There was also smoke coming from the fire over on Graves Creek near its juncture with Lolo Creek. I took readings on both fires and reported to Carroll.

"Both Darrell and Clarence are down at the Graves Creek fire," he said. "Ross and I are the only ones here at the station, so you're going to have to take the fire below you."

"But who'll watch the store while I'm gone?" I asked.

And he said, "Don't worry. I'll send Ross up to relieve you as soon as Darrell returns. So get on it fast!" And then as an after-thought, "The fire should be near the road, so take your car."

I grabbed the firepack, hurried down the trail to my car, put the fire pack in the rumble seat, and raced down the road. I came to the fire in less than a mile, just off the road as Carroll had said. It was a little over an acre and creeping slowly uphill. I started at the bottom of the fire and scraped a shallow trench up the right side with my fire pack shovel, around the top and down the other side. The idea is to pinch the fire off before it can take off.

I took a "five" back from the fire where I could cool off. It was still chilly at that elevation early in the morning. Then I started around again, deepening the trench, keeping an eye on my back to make sure the fire didn't jump the trench and trap me. I was part way up the right side when Ross arrived. He jumped in ahead of me. He had the knowing moves of an experienced fire fighter. He fought the fire like he was calming down one of his balky mules — smoothly, surely and unhurriedly. Go at it too hard and fast and you'll soon burn yourself out. We sowed cool earth on the hot spots, tangles of logs that give off furnace heat. You keep your left shoulder and arm up to protect your face and neck from flying sparks. Your felt hat and heavy gloves protect your head and hands.

When we completed the second pass, we took another five-minute break. The fire appeared to be pretty much under control. Ross said, "Why don't you go back to the lookout and report the situation here to Carroll. I'll mop up. Tell him I won't be too much longer."

At the lookout, I noticed there was more smoke coming up at the Graves Creek fire, and when I reported to Carroll what Ross had said, I mentioned the smoke on Graves Creek. Carroll said keep an eye on the fire below you for a few days. As the day wore on, black smoke boiled up from Graves Creek, but I figured Clarence was down there and knew what was going on, so I didn't call the station.

A few days later, Clarence came up to the lookout on an inspection trip and chewed me out. "Didn't you see black smoke coming up from the fire," he bawled. Considering his size and professional wrestling background, I thought it only prudent to appear contrite, respectful and mumbled, "Yes, sir."

"You should call the station when a fire turns black," he chewed on. "I only had forty men and I needed sixty. I had to leave the fire and go back to the station for reinforcements, and while I was gone, it blew out the top and nearly took Blue Mountain. We had a hell of a time containing it."

"Holy smokes," I said. "I had no idea, Clarence. I did report to Carroll that there was more smoke coming up when I got back from my fire along about noon. I'm sorry."

"Well," he said cooling down, "next time be sure you call when you see black smoke coming up."

And then he said, "We'll rack that one up to experience. Why don't you go down and get some fresh spring water. I've got a couple of steaks and fresh vegetables in the car, and while you're gone I'll cook up a batch of biscuits."

Clarence's biscuits were light, fluffy, halfway between a biscuit and a cookie. There was water in the backpack cooling out under the eaves, but I didn't question the necessity for fresh water. Clarence always got you out of the way on some pretext or other when he made his biscuits. I think it may have been a closely guarded family recipe.

Black Dog and I ambled down to the spring. I told Black Dog we'd give the secretive old bastard plenty of time to make his biscuits. As we climbed up the rock to the lookout on the return trip, I could smell the sweet aroma of Clarence's biscuits.

Clarence filled one frying pan with the steaks, another with potatoes and onions, and a pot of fresh peas. Biscuits, steaks, potatoes, onions and fresh peas are very special when you haven't had them in some time, and I told him so. Clarence was proud of his cooking capabilities and he swelled up, beamed, forgot to be sore, and we were friends.

After lunch he made an inspection of the lookout — windows, floors, stove (stoves must be black from regular applications of stove black), firepack, exterior paint, weather instruments, outhouse and garbage pit. I thought I'd get chewed out over the condition of the garbage pit, but he didn't have any suggestions to keep the grizzly out and passed over that.

He was most concerned with the weather instruments. I had the feeling Clarence enjoyed grilling me on the proper use of these instruments — the executive officer inspecting one of the troops.

One morning Black Dog and I were outside poking about among the rocks. They were of sedimentary origin, laid down by seas millions of years ago. There were inch-thick flakes here and there that the winter freezing and thawing had peeled off. Some of them had fossils of small sea creatures on their surface. It was fun to poke about looking for different kinds of fossils.

I caught a movement out of the corner of my eye, and there was our grizzly bear ambling across the rocky talus slope below us. The hair stood up on Black Dog's back and she uttered a low growl. I quickly clamped a hand over her nose, but the grizzly had either heard Black Dog or caught our scent on a vagrant breeze. It looked up at us, swung its head back and forth as if mulling over whether to come up or not. We remained perfectly still. But in my mind I was thinking of picking up Black Dog, dashing to the lookout, pushing Black Dog up on the shutters that extended horizontally out over the windows, grabbing the double bitted ax by the door, and climbing up after her.

I thought to myself, If the grizzly tries to climb up after us, I'll split its head open with the ax. But fortunately the bear turned, moved slowly across the rocky slope, and disappeared into the forest.

During the day telephones were to be used for Forest Service business only. But in the evenings we could talk with the other lookouts. Dewey was on the other end of my line at Skookum Butte, and often we'd pick up the phone and talk. Invariably when I'd ask him what he'd been up to, he'd say "I baked a cake today", chocolate, lemon, whatever. I don't think Dewey had many cakes as a child, nor as a migrant worker in the Arizona citrus fields.

Like most men's bull sessions, the conversation got around to sex eventually. There were the persistent rumors of butterflies of the night servicing the lookouts and beautiful women hikers extending favors to others. When I'd ask Dewey if he had been so favored he'd reply, "Not lucky today. Guess they haven't heard of

the Skookum Butte stud." I think the rumors were the wishful thinking of lonely men.

Occasionally I would see one of the old Ford Tri-Motor planes lumbering up the Lolo Valley and over Lolo Pass, carrying supplies and smoke jumpers to fires in the remote regions of the Powell Ranger District. Powell was one of the largest ranger districts, over 400,000 acres of the Lochsa and Selway wilderness. The smoke jumper was a relatively new innovation for getting fire fighters to a fire while it was still small. It was especially effective in reaching into remote trackless areas.

These planes, though fifteen to twenty years old, were ideally suited to the task. They could be flown low and slow over a fire allowing the smoke jumpers to parachute close to the fire. The smoke jumpers were heavily padded, wore face masks, and were equipped with rope to lower themselves to the ground if caught in a tree. Supplies and fire fighting equipment were then parachuted to them.

I did not realize it at the time, but what I was seeing was the passing of the lookout era in the Forest Service. The airplane was to supplant the lookout for spotting fires, and the lookout buildings were to be torn down. A few remain to be used as shelter by hunters, fishermen and hikers.

The lookout era was one of unhurried time. You watched the day begin in the East, pass lazily overhead and disappear in a magnificent display of color in the West. Time, the most precious commodity of all, was yours to spend in large quantities. The days blended together, one scarcely different from another. Like so many other things, the lookout era existed but a brief time in the history of the West.

Part Three

TWO FISHING STORIES

Chapter **12**

SUNDANCE

We would not have met Dr. Gunn if Grandpa had not hooked his left index finger with a number 14 caddis fly instead of a plump cutthroat trout. On this particular day in late June, Grandpa and I and my two sons, Rob and Tom, had been casting our flys upon the waters of Lost Horse Creek in the panhandle of Idaho.

But then Grandpa made the cast mentioned above and the hook being buried beyond the barb, we had to pull up stakes and seek medical help.

The drive back to our cottage on Priest Lake was the usual entertaining and animated event Grandpa always made of it. Grandpa was a church-going, God-fearing man, yet he feared no car anytime, anywhere. He delighted in the over-the-hill and around-the-curve passes, and the difficult but thrilling forzado de pecho, or forced pass executed on a one-lane road with left hand only, while right hand is used to wave reassuringly to party passed. The boys loved Grandpa's driving and more than once said it was more fun to ride with Grandpa than ride the loop-the-loop or devil's roller coaster.

As we approached the cottage, Grandpa suddenly turned to us and admonished, "Now, not a word to Grandma. We can't worry her in her condition." Grandma had high blood pressure.

Grandpa's feet scarcely touched the front porch before he was calling for Grandma and showing her his wounded finger and asking, "Is there a doctor in the bay?" Grandma took a quick appraisal of the situation and put it down as not much and said, "I have heard there is a doctor staying down at the resort."

Grandpa and I soon located the good doctor, Dr. Gunn. At the moment he was wearing a rumpled sweatshirt, baggy cotton summer pants, sneakers and a billed cap. He quickly demonstrated his medical skills, dispelling any doubts his attire had raised, by snipping off the eye of the fly and pushing the remainder through the flesh and out.

During the course of the operation, we learned that Dr. Gunn was from north of the border. I noticed a beautifully aged, split-cane rod resting at the door that indicated this was a fly fisherman of some capability. I said with poorly disguised envy, "That's a beautiful rod you have there."

"It was handed down to me by my Scottish grandfather," Dr. Gunn said. "He fished highland streams with it, and I still use it on open rivers and mountain lakes, waters where there is small chance of damaging it."

He handed it to me. "Feel the action."

And then he inquired innocently, "How did you do today?" I admitted that we had taken several substantial cutthroat trout but was rather vague as to where we had taken them.

"What do I owe you?" Grandpa broke in impatiently, reaching for his checkbook.

"The word here at the resort is that you people know where the fish are," the good doctor ventured humbly. "Why don't you just take me fishing with you next time?"

Normally Grandpa would as soon give up the key to his lockbox as divulge the location of good trout-holding water, but in this case Dr. Gunn had been so humble and wistful in his approach and Grandpa, being a man close with his checkbook, accepted the proposition.

"We'll be fishing Sundance three days from now," Grandpa offered. "It's a tiny mountain lake that's lightly fished. Lies in Washington just over the Idaho border in a remote area. It's accessible only from Idaho. So not too many Washington people fish it. And few Idaho people fish it because the out-of-state license is steep and there are plenty of places to fish in Idaho. Incidentally, do you have a Washington fishing license?"

"No, just the Idaho license."

"Well it's too far to drive to Washington for the license," Grandpa decided. "The boys can fish Sundance Lake. You and I can fish Sundance Creek on the Idaho side. They're both loaded with lunker cutthroat that run up Sundance Creek this time of year to spawn." Dr. Gunn was beginning to show the early symptoms of trout fever.

"We'll pick you up around 7," Grandpa continued. "Sundance is a fairly long drive on a gravel logging road."

On the way to Sundance two days later, it was clear the good doctor had been festering over Grandpa's casual statement about the lunker cutthroat trout.

"You say Sundance trout are of lunker proportions," he prodded Grandpa.

"Yes, they are weighty," Grandpa confirmed. "You see Sundance Creek is a torrent this time of year from the snow-melt. There are also numerous low falls the fish have to contend with, so only the largest mature spawners get this far.

"Sundance Creek has been open to fishing only two years," Grandpa continued. "Before that it was always closed to protect the spawning runs. So you'll be fishing virtually virgin waters."

At the mention of virgin waters, the good doctor, in mounting excitement, asked tremulously, "What flies do these, ah, lunkers take?"

"They're not at all finicky," Grandpa explained matter-of-factly. "They'll take anything with a little red on it ibis, royal coachman, parmachene belle."

"Fabulous," the good doctor murmured.

"I must warn you," Grandpa said. "We do have a pretty rugged hike in and out of the Sundance Canyon. But you'll find it's well worth the effort."

By the time we let Grandpa and Dr. Gunn out, the good doctor was anticipating the thrill of a lifetime. And he was to have it, but not quite in the way he expected.

Meanwhile, the boys and I backtracked to the turnout at Sundance Lake. They say it was named Sundance, because when the sun slices through the hole in the giant trees at just the right angle and there is a ripple on the water, the light leaps and dances across the gem-like wave facets.

I first fished Sundance in the 30s when it was a twelve mile hike over the divide from Stagger Inn, a forest service line cabin. It had changed little since then. The access trail showed greater usage but the ancient, water-logged raft and pole that anchored it to the shore were still in the little cove to the left.

To fish Sundance, you have three choices: You attempt to stay afloat on the raft; you balance on one of the slippery logs that reach beyond the dropoff; you wade and use the rollcast as the trees grow up to the water's edge and the water quickly deepens offshore. Any of the three can subject you to a dunking in the icy water. Rob opted for wading, Tom the log, and I mounted the raft.

I poled, then paddled the old raft out past the shade cast by the great pine and fir. It was warm out of the shade. I was content to let the raft drift, to peer into the depths for the lunker trout, to listen to the wind soughing lazily through the tree tops, and for a few brief moments to float free of time and even the necessity to fish.

Then I heard a splashing and looked over in time to see Rob reach into the water at his feet, then lift a heavy cutthroat for me to see. He had been roll casting to a tree recently fallen into the water that still had needles on the branches. Rob at nine was already showing signs of becoming top rod in the family, and it had been some feat to keep a trout of such proportions from hanging up in the tree branches.

"How big?" I called over.

"Eighteen or better." Then he released him — family rule with spawning fish.

"What did he take?"

"Montana nymph."

Adrenalin now flowing, I started to tie on a Montana nymph, but noticed that the sun had now reached into the little cove and there was a dimpling on the water. Rob had been in the shade, and the trout there were nymphing. I tied on an Adams and laid it along the logs that had piled up in the cove.

I retrieved but a few feet of line when the first fish rose to the fly. I struck too fast and missed but continued the retrieve as I had seen several good trout dart out from the logs. The Adams moved but a few feet when I had a second rise. This time I slowed the strike and was tight to him.

He was heavy and forced his way back under the logs. Their limbs had long ago dropped off, so I was content to lay back and apply pressure. His tactics were not spectacular, the usual conservative underwater cutthroat runs and surges with the ever present danger and concern for a broken tippet or hook pull-out.

I edged him out from the logs, and he immediately dove under the raft. Then I stepped too close to the old raft's edge, and it dipped under water. I scrambled to mid-ship, and it righted. But the rod now dipped under the raft giving a compass reading indicating the trout's location as directly off the opposite side. I worked the rod around the end of the raft and found that I was still tied to the devious devil.

I snubbed him up tightly and he again dove under the raft, but this time I stayed safely mid-ship. A bit more pressure and I finally had him in hand. His throat slashes were bright red and his belly pink...a native cutthroat in full mating colors. I released him, watched him hesitate and then drift off into deeper water.

Meanwhile, Tom had moved out on the log jam at the outlet from Sundance, and with open space for a backcast had been casting well out into the lake. I watched both boys catch and release several heavy fish, and then it was time to pick up Grandpa and Dr. Gunn.

We had driven but a short way when we met them trudging up the road. They were redfaced, streaked with dust, fanning themselves with their hats. Dr. Gunn's shirt was torn.

We had agreed to pick them up where we had left them, and they had now walked a couple of miles from that point. I was getting bad vibes, a vague feeling that something was very wrong. I felt concern and worry for Grandpa, but other than being a bit more stooped and grim, he seemed quite healthy.

"Are you OK?" I asked and then added, "How was the fishing?"

"OK on the first count," Grandpa said dryly. "Negative on the second."

"We hit Sundance at a little falls and there were beautiful big cutthroat leaping it," Dr. Gunn put in wistfully. "We were setting up our rods when two lumberjacks came along and told us the stream was closed."

"They showed us a sign tacked to a tree," Grandpa interjected bitterly. "They said the warden had caught two fellows last week, and the judge fined them $500 each and seized their equipment."

"At least you still have your heirloom rod and $500, Dr. Gunn," I offered lamely, attempting to take the edge off his disappointment.

But we were in for further excitement on the drive back. Grandpa had taken over the helm and just executed a two-car, around-the-curve-and-over-the-hill pass, in a narrow canyon, when we heard a quavering gasp from Dr. Gunn's sector of the car.

"There's a logging truck bearing down on us from behind," and then seconds later, "My God, it's out of control."

Logging trucks, of course, will flatten the ordinary car as a heel will a beer can, and at this precise moment our right front tire blew. Grandpa quickly executed a brilliant pase de pecho on the shoulder, a side-stepping maneuver used to liberate oneself from the charge of a bull or vehicle. The logging truck burned by, coming to a stop down the canyon.

"Smooth move, Gramps," Rob said in open admiration.

"Brilliant," Dr. Gunn agreed somewhat shaken, never having been exposed to a driver of Grandpa's stature.

We had changed the tire and were moving briskly down the road again when suddenly muffled sobs rose from Dr. Gunn's sector of the car. I wondered if he were suffering latent shock from the near accident.

"Are you all right, doctor?" I asked sympathetically.

"Perfect," he responded gleefully. "You've put me on a closed stream. Nearly had me fined $500 with the loss of an heirloom fly rod. You nearly killed me by a logging truck. Don't you have some other diabolical treats up your sleeve?"

"Indeed we do," I bandied back. "I was just now thinking the golden trout of Hunt Lake might offer just the antidote to today's expedition."

"Spare me," the good doctor chortled.

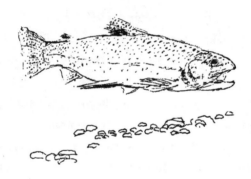

Chapter 13

GUNN'S BEND

It was little wonder Dr. Gunn was skeptical when we offered to take him fishing to Hunt Lake for golden trout. After all, the expedition to "Sundance" had been a disaster. Only Grandpa's superb driving had averted a tragedy.

"Are you sure this Hunt Lake is open to fishing?" the good doctor asked guardedly.

"Absolutely. No question," I parried.

"And does it have fish in it?"

"Chock-full of golden trout," I warmed to the subject. "They were planted a few years ago, and I hear they have grown to generous proportions."

Faith slowly returning, Dr. Gunn said, "I'm a sucker for wild goose chases. Count me in."

It was a crisp, chilly mountain morning when Dr. Gunn, my two sons, Tom and Rob, and I took off shortly after sunrise for

Hunt Lake. It lies just under the crest of the Selkirk Range on the east shore of Priest Lake in northern Idaho. Grandpa had turned down the trip.

"At my age, seventy-five," he'd said, "you're not going to get me to traipse around those mountain peaks." Frankly, I think Grandma had put her little foot down, which at times could be more forceful than a lumberjack's caulked White logging boots.

Steam was rising off the Priest River as we followed it down to the Dickensheet Road, which would take us over to the east shore. The river here is a series of long deep pools interspersed with stretches of riffles, heavy rapids, great boulders and occasionally where the river dips downward sharply, rooster tails. At Binarch rapids, where Binarch Creek joins the river, there is an old Indian camping grounds on a high bank that gives a splendid view of the river. Over the years it has been the setting for numerous picture postcards.

Dr. Gunn remarked, "That quiet water, just below where Binarch Creek joins the river, should hold a big trout or two."

"In the old days, yes," I replied. "Jim Low, a homesteader, once told me of having caught all the sixteen inch cutthroat trout he could carry, with just a willow pole, short length of line, gut leader, snelled hook and grasshoppers at this very spot.

"The Priest River used to be one of the great cutthroat fisheries in the West," I continued, "But now along the blacktop the river's too accessible and it's fished out. If you want to catch trout of any consequence, you need to hike back into remote areas."

"Too bad," Dr. Gunn said wistfully, "It's so beautiful I'd just like to lay a fly out and watch it sail down the currents."

Soon we reached the Dickensheet Road and crossed over to the east shore. From here, a Forest Service road, which is basically a one-lane goat track with turn-outs took us up to Camels Prairie

Lookout, jumping off point for Hunt Lake.

This section of the Selkirks has always had a large population of both grizzly and black bear and remains today one of the four places in the lower forty-eight where there are still grizzlies. As we rounded one particularly sharp bend, a small cinnamon bear scampered across the road ahead, and we stopped and watched until it disappeared downridge. It was an especially light, iridescent color — rather ghost-like — and gave me an eerie feeling.

"Would you say that's a good or bad omen, doctor?" I asked.

"Gave me a creepy feeling," the good doctor replied. "But I would say the gods favor this trip!"

From Camel's Prairie, we followed a Forest Service trail down into the headwaters of the south fork of Hunt Creek. Then we lost the trail in a maze of under growth and slashings from a recent logging operation.

"At one time, there was another Forest Service trail that ran along the top of that ridge ahead. It would take us to the headwall overlooking Hunt Lake," I offered. "If we can get through this brush and slashings it should be easy going."

"Let's give it a try," Dr. Gunn and the boys chorused.

We fought the buckbrush and walked logs up to the ridge top but never found the trail. It had long since disappeared under fallen trees and huckleberry bushes. However, the terrain was now open, park-like, sparsely forested with whitebark pine. The forest floor was a great garden of blooming bear grass.

We followed the ridge upwards. At first it rose gently and the walking was easy, but then we reached the headwall and the grade rose abruptly. The air became thinner as we climbed higher and higher. At 6,000 feet, Rob who was nine and Tom thirteen were having a hard time breathing the thin air. The sun was now hot and heavy, and we tied our sweaters around our waists. We stopped every hundred yards to catch our breath. Finally we broke free at timberline on a knife-like ridge overlooking Hunt Lake.

It lay in a great cirque a thousand feet below. It was a deep blue-violet indicating considerable depth, elliptical in shape and perhaps three-quarters of a mile in length. Huge gray granite slabs that had tumbled from the cirque walls over eons of time bordered the lake with the exception of the outlet where green grasses and yellow splashes of alpine lilies grew. Fingers of alpine fir and whitebark pine reached up the ravines of the near vertical slopes. Across from us, the smooth granite face of Gunsight Peak rose above us.

The only visible route down was to cross a snowfield on our right along which tardy alpine lilies grew. Then down a chute to the shoreline.

At first we could lower ourselves by clutching dwarf whitebark pine growing out of the cracks and patches of dirt. But as we got closer to the lake, we came upon boulders, some the size of houses, and had to crawl over and around them to the water's edge.

We spread out around the lake and quickly set up our fly rods. The water near shore was a light green but very quickly became the blue-violet as it deepened. The surface of the lake was flat and glassy, and I watched for cruising, feeding fish but did not see so much as a fingerling.

I tied on a Montana nymph and cast out into the darker water, let the nymph sink for several minutes and then started my retrieve expecting any minute to see a flash of gold following it. I'd been so confident that in an area so remote the action would be swift and sure.

After several casts, I changed to the ever reliable gold-ribbed hares ear, then the bitch creek, followed by assorted streamers, the muddler minnow, a black ant, a red ant and as the day warmed a Joe's hopper.

Then I moved up to where a small inlet bubbled into the lake, and although I had not seen a rise nor a mayfly of any description proceeded to lay out a series of dry flies at its mouth — adams, dark cahil, mosquito, parmacheene belle, black gnat, and in desperation a stone fly. I reasoned that at this elevation, like the tardy alpine lilies, the stone flies might just be coming into season. I didn't raise a trout. No one did.

We finally met for lunch. We sat on one of the house size granite slabs watching for a rise and peering into the deep but crystal clear water for a flash of a trout. The trout for all we could tell could very well be lunching on nymphs at mid-lake.

We were all beginning to get an uneasy feeling about the lake, and Dr. Gunn was the first to express our fears. "You know," he said, "located at this elevation, this lake could freeze solid in a severe winter. I've seen it happen in the Canadian Rockies."

"Or the fish may not be feeding," I countered. "Trout in mountain lakes can be finicky feeders, you know."

Dr. Gunn dipped a tin cup into the lake, took a deep swallow and said, "Well, no one has so much as seen a trout. I'm more inclined to think it's barren".

The evidence was on the doctor's side, but I couldn't pack it in. I wanted my first golden trout badly, and I suggested, "Let's give it another hour, and then we'll have to pull out if we're to get back at a reasonable hour."

Even as the afternoon warmed, a hatch did not materialize nor did we see any rises. We continued fishing blindly for another hour and then gave it up.

During lunch, we had noticed a hand-over-hand route that led to a ravine, not visible from the ridge top, that would take us close to where we had first looked down on Hunt Lake.

We opted for this route and shortly after we topped out and had started down the other side, we stumbled upon a trail that led in the general direction of where we had left the car. We could chance an unknown trail or soon be fighting our way through known logging slashings. We took the trail. It took us through acres and acres of salal brush, skirted the logged-over area and finally dumped us out on a slight rise overlooking the car.

We had left the car in the open, and the metal and Naugahyde seats were hot to the touch. We opened the windows and took our time stowing the gear in the trunk. Then we drove down into the heavy timber where it was cooler.

Dr. Gunn had been quiet for some time, and I was feeling sorry for him and let down myself. I had wanted badly to show him the golden trout of Hunt Lake and regain face I had lost at Sundance.

The boys, too, had been subdued for some time when Rob suddenly spoke up, "I guess you and Dr. Gunn misread the bear omen," he needled.

"Well, Rob," I replied, "We didn't catch a golden trout, but we did see one of the truly beautiful spots of the world. It's the kind of place you can store away and take out when everything is going wrong. You can go back to this day, see the snowfield with alpine lilies coming up along the edges, make the rugged descent to the lake, climb over the big boulders along the shore, lay a fly out into the clear water, and look up at Gunsight. You'll see every detail so clearly. You'll even feel the haunting loneliness and peacefulness, and your problems will not seem so important."

Rob giggled, "That sounds like it came right from Grandpa's 'chopping block lecture series.' "

"Your Grandpa's a smart man," I replied.

"Good therapy," Dr. Gunn put in.

The mountain tops about us were still bathed in light as we drove along the Priest River. But in the valley, light was fading fast, and the great pine and fir and cedar were beginning to fade into a black wall on either side of the road. At the final bend before the river leaves the road, we saw a dimpling on the water. The good doctor shouted, "Stop the car. The river's alive with feeding trout."

I knew it was nothing but a school of squawfish on a feeding binge but thought it best to humor him at this point and pulled off the road. He quickly set up the heirloom rod and asked,
"Aren't you going to join me?"

"No," I said, "you deserve all the fun."

We watched as the doctor waded out into the river. He laid out long, lazy, beautiful casts and soon was into a heavy squawfish as I knew he would be. The fish moved slowly back and forth in the strong current at mid-stream, and any moment I expected to see it surface and roll over belly up. But then as the minutes passed, and the fish held stubbornly in mid-stream, I had an uneasy feeling. At last he worked the fish into the shallows at his feet, reached down, and lifted the dripping fish triumphantly over his head. It was a silvery cutthroat trout of some size.

I felt a twinge of conscience for having set him up but nothing serious enough to prevent me from bolting to the river and asking, "What did you take him on?"

"Female lady beaverkill with yellow egg sack."

I could now see that the air over the river was filled with small mayflies. There were even a few on the doctor's cap and shoulders.

"If you don't have any, I have a good supply," he offered.

Feeling somewhat sheepish, I nevertheless graciously accepted three, and the boys and I spread out along a run above the doctor. There was hardly a moment when someone did not have a trout on, and there were times when all four of us were into good fish.

It was a festival; it was the good old days, and the most unbelievable aspect of the whole thing was the number and variety of fish back in the river. We caught cutthroat, nothing the size of Dr. Gunn's first fish, but plump acceptable specimens. We caught rainbow trout. And we caught firm, pan size, succulent whitefish. The fish had sneaked back into their old haunts unbeknownst to us.

Finally it became too dark to see, and the action stopped. We lined up on a log looking out over the river, quietly savoring the moment, not ready to give it up just yet.

I noticed out of the corner of my eye that the doctor was slumped forward, elbows resting on knees, face drawn, tired. He looked satisfied but humble. I felt very warm toward him and grateful.

"You know, boys," I said, breaking the silence. "We ought to name this Gunn's Bend."

The good doctor declined demurely, but to this very day we always refer to that particular stretch of river as Gunn's Bend.

EPILOGUE

ROSS MIDDLEMIST SERVED IN THE FIRST MARINE AMPHIBIOUS Company in World War II and was involved in the landings on Saipain and Tinian. After the war he returned to Lolo, Mont., and again worked for the Forest Service as packer on the Lolo Ranger District. He married a lovely lady, Frances Holmes, a school teacher in Lolo. She also served in the armed services as a WAVE, stationed in Washington, D.C. They bought a thirty-two acre ranch which has become downtown Lolo. Ross rose to become Fire Control Officer for the Missoula Ranger District. They still live in a comfortable ranch house in Lolo and are active in their church and in community affairs.

Dewey Duffel also served in the armed services in the South Pacific. Evidently the lessons he learned in the gambling parlors of Missoula and vicinity paid off because he returned to Montana after the war not only with a sizable discharge check, but also substantial winnings from gambling while in the service. Dewey bought a stump ranch along the Pend Oreille River west of Thompson Falls, Mont. He married a lady named Marge. I do not know her last name. They eked out a living from the ranch. When the Montana Power and Light bought his and other ranchers land along the Pend Oreille for the Noxon Dam, Dewey bought a sporting goods store in Thompson Falls with the proceeds. He managed it successfully for several years. In later years he developed emphysema and moved to Phoenix, Ariz. He died there in the early 1980s.

ABOUT THE AUTHOR

THOMAS F. LACY WAS BORN IN SPOKANE, WASH., IN 1918, AND grew up listening to stories of the Inland Northwest's frontier days told by the old logging barons, cattlemen, wheat farmers and lawmen who settled it. He attended schools in Spokane, and passed summers at the family cabin at Priest Lake. In 1940 he graduated from the University of Idaho with a bachelor's degree in forestry. In summers he worked for the Forest Service, first with the Blister Rust Corps in the St. Joe River country and then at the Lolo Ranger District on trail crew, lookouts and as dispatcher.

The Forest Service was not hiring full-time workers, so he attended and graduated in 1942 from the Harvard Graduate School of Business. World War II was under way, and that fall he enlisted in the Air Corps at Fort George Wright in Spokane and ultimately served at a regional office of the Material Command before his discharge in August 1945 with rank of First Lieutenant.

After the war he worked for an advertising agency in Detroit. He opened his own agency in Ann Arbor, Mich., three years later. "What I enjoyed most was sitting in front of a typewriter writing advertising copy," he recalls. "I dreamed of writing something more lasting, something of value. This book is the culmination of that dream." He returns to his family cabin on Priest Lake each summer, still hiking and fishing the high country.